LAWNS

LAWNS

MATT TEMPLETON

DAVID AND CHARLES
NEWTON ABBOT   LONDON
NORTH POMFRET (VT)   VANCOUVER

For
JOYCE

ISBN 0 7153 6818 4
Library of Congress Catalog Card Number 74-20461

Computer typeset in 11 on 13pt Plantin
by Input Typesetting Limited   London
and printed in Great Britain
by Biddles Limited   Guildford
for David & Charles (Publishers) Limited
Brunel House   Newton Abbot   Devon

Published in the United States of America
by David & Charles Inc
North Pomfret   Vermont 05053   USA

Published in Canada
by Douglas David & Charles Limited
1875 Welch Street   North Vancouver   BC

Contents

List of Illustrations

All the illustrations, with the exception of Fig 2, are by Marguerite Miles.

Preface

From medieval times, when impoverished gentry discovered that seeds and turves from the pasture were a cheap and easy way of beautifying the ground around buildings, lawns have fulfilled a multitude of different functions. The billiard-table smoothness of Restoration bowling greens, the cluttered formality of seventeenth century formal gardens and the carefully landscaped expansiveness of 'Capability' Brown's parkland were as much dependent for their charm and effectiveness on large areas of grass as is the modern suburban garden.

Though, as is the case today, economy may have been the motive for transplanting the coarse, broad-leaved grasses that constituted the first lawns, those were more feudal and more spacious days. Now time is too precious to devote to lawn upkeep, be it your own or anyone else's, and land is too expensive to put it all out to grass. One factor, however, remains unchanged – the great number of purposes for which lawns are made. The long-suffering green behind the house that must be part paddock, part football pitch, drying area and kitchen garden, is becoming increasingly common, but there are still thousands of acres of public parkland, tennis courts, croquet lawns, bowling greens and, surprisingly enough, set pieces of ornamental turf, surrounded by decorative beds and borders.

The continuing experimenting by plant breeders over the years has produced grasses for every situation and ever better methods of maintaining the lawns made from them. Such a plethora of knowledge is often as confusing for the park attendant as for the amateur gardener. I have tried, therefore, to answer all the questions that could be asked about lawns in as simple a way as possible, whilst drawing on the most up to date information. My text is based on the latest technical advances but, I hope, presented with the minimum of technicalities. This is not a book to be read from end to end, but one that can be dipped into time and again to give quick answers and

9

results. The material is presented in alphabetical order so that, unlike most of the presently available lawn literature, it is not necessary to wade through a whole chapter in order to find the required information.

From these pages you will discover that the most expensive, and most crucial, item in making a lawn is time. But it is time well spent and a worthwhile investment. Once a lawn is established the continuing outlay becomes a matter of minutes and pennies rather than hours and pounds. With the increase in scientific knowledge about turf and the development of new techniques to maintain it in prime condition, it is now possible to use time very profitably. I trust that this volume will help thousands of gardeners to do just that.

A-Z of Lawns

Achillea millefolium See Yarrow

Acidity See Lime, pH, Soil Testing

Aeration
Most lawns receive a lot of use during the spring and summer months with a tendency of the surface to compact and form an increasingly impervious layer of soil around the grass roots. Neglect of this condition only causes the hazard to increase, rains cannot penetrate easily, plant foods are not absorbed and over a period the soil becomes sour.

Regular aeration every autumn is therefore most beneficial; it conditions the turf and helps heavy soils to drain better in addition to providing an opportunity to add organic materials as a top dressing (qv) to keep the sward healthy and flourishing. Aeration also tends to stimulate roots to grow deeper and so enables the turf to withstand drought better during the following summer.

SCARIFYING Aeration of the immediate turf surface and is best carried out with a sprung wire rake to remove dead vegetation, decayed grass cuttings and other debris. The operation also eliminates excessive fibre and breaks up the mat so often caused by heavy use of turf. Lawns should be scarified at least once a year during the spring but preferably at monthly intervals during the growing season.

SPIKING An operation which involves aeration to a greater depth, and can bring about quite remarkable improvements of the turf.

On light soils, use a garden fork, pushing it into the ground to a depth of 4in. Move it backwards and forwards, and sideways too, to increase the size of hole each tine makes. Withdraw the fork, and walking backwards repeat the same procedure, some 6-9in away. Keep the fork in a vertical position when pushing it into the soil and withdrawing it, or the turf is inclined to lift and disturb the roots.

Fig 1 Using a hollow-tine fork

A special hollow-tined fork is needed for the same operation on heavier soils. These are constructed like garden forks but have three or more spring loaded hollow tines, each of which makes a hole in the ground equivalent to the thickness of a pencil. As the tool is withdrawn from the soil, the springs eject the core of soil on to the turf. These cores are best swept up unless one of the 'de luxe' tools which incorporate a special soil core collector is used. For the larger turf areas one of the many new tools, some motorised, that have been introduced during recent years, may be useful (Fig 1).

Agricultural Chemicals Approval Scheme

This voluntary scheme for insecticides, weedkillers and fungicides is administered by the Ministry of Agriculture.

Some manufacturers submit their pesticide products for approval and if granted, the product label carries the government's approval mark (Fig 2). Approval is only granted if the material is reasonably effective against the weeds and pests it claims to control and provided it carries a label (the text of which must also be approved) which states the ingredients in addition to the recommended dosage and necessary precautions.

Prior to approval, pesticides have first to be cleared by the voluntary Pesticides Safety Precautions Scheme. Fertilisers are not covered by either scheme and fertiliser/weedkiller mixtures can consequently not be submitted for approval.

AGRICULTURAL CHEMICALS APPROVAL SCHEME

Fig 2 Agricultural Chemicals approval mark

Agropyron repens See Couch

Agrostis

A group of hardy, fine-leaved, stoloniferous (qv) grasses present in most fine turf. See Bent Grasses.

Algae

A low form of flowerless plant, similar to fungus, but unlike the latter, it contains chlorophyll. Usually found in damp situations created either through lack of drainage, or excess consolidation of the soil. Overhanging trees dripping on to the ground, or heavy soils, also encourage its spread. It usually takes the form of dark, slimy blue-green patches. Control can be obtained by watering the affected area and surrounds with sulphate of iron solution at the rate of 1oz in 1gal of water per 2sq yd.

If the incidence of algae is not very serious, permanent control can be achieved by aeration and repeated top dressing with sand to lighten the surface layer of the soil; continued persistence of algae in spite of these measures can only be alleviated by attention to the drainage system.

Copper sulphate solution is occasionally mistakenly advised for the control of algae in grass.

Alkalinity See Lime, pH, Soil Testing

Ammonium Sulphamate
A translocated and soil-acting weedkiller usually available in the form of soluble crystals; useful for the destruction of tree stumps (qv).

Ammonium Sulphate See Sulphate of Ammonia

Annual Blue Grass See Meadow Grasses

Annual Meadow Grass See Meadow Grasses

Anthemis nobilis Chamomile See Grass Substitutes

Ants
These can be a nuisance in turf established on light, sandy soils. The ants throw up small mounds of soil which disfigure the lawn and are tiresome when mowing and rolling. BHC provides satisfactory control and may be applied at the rate recommended by the manufacturers either as dust or in a liquid suspension, preferably the latter.

Aphanes arvensis See Parsley Piert

Armeria maritima See Sea Pink

Asexual
Sexless or the propagation of plants by vegetative means instead of

growing them from seed. See Vegetative Reproduction.

Auricle
A hook-like protruberance on some grasses at the bottom of the leaf-blade where it joins the sheath.

Bacon-and-Eggs See Bird's-foot Trefoil

Banks and Slopes
Avoid them if possible as they are difficult to establish and maintain. Even moderate rainfall tends to wash soil, seeds and fertilisers to the bottom of the incline, mowing is made difficult and virtually impossible on the steepest slopes.

If the natural contours of the site demand the construction of banks, try to keep their incline at no more than 30° and preferably at 20° although the more shallow the slope, the bigger the area. Shallow slopes drain less quickly than really steep banks which, particularly on lighter soils, may show symptoms of drought even during damp weather.

Both the base and top of banks should be rounded off with gentle curves to avoid scalping the turf when mowing. Use 1in mesh polypropylene yarn to ease construction of the very steep slopes; it minimises soil movement, combats erosion and permits the grass to take root without undue disturbance. Stretch the net all over the previously prepared sloping area and secure firmly with U-hooks. Then seed in the usual way. When the grass is first cut, set the cutting knives at their maximum height, watch for snags and re-pin any exposed netting. Polypropylene mesh can also be used to prevent erosion on already turfed banks. Spread it in the usual way, pin firmly, and permit the grass to grow well through the net before commencing to mow. The most suitable type of mowers for cutting grass on steep banks are the light weight rotaries that move over the turf on a cushion of air.

Bare Patches
There are innumerable explanations that could account for their presence on turf. Mechanical wear by children's feet underneath the

garden swing, the daily tramping of the postman and newspaper delivery boy cutting across the lawn on their shortest way to the front door. The only long term solution is to set some stone slabs underneath the swing and construct a path for the postman; or change the shape of the lawn.

If the lawn is uneven, turf is apt to be scalped on the high-lying spots by the mower. To correct this, cut the turf around the high spot with a moonshaped turfing iron; gently peel back the turf, remove excess soil, roll the turf back and fill the cracks with a mixture of peat and sand to assist the seams to knit quickly.

Pests and disease as well as lack of aeration could also be responsible. See Chafer Grubs, Dollar Spot, Fusarium Patch, Aeration and Drainage.

Bellis perennis ´See Daisy

Bent Grasses
A collective name for grasses of the genus *Agrostis*, which includes brown top, or common bent, *A. tenuis;* creeping bent, *A. stolonifera;*

Ligule

Fig 3 Brown Top

16

and velvet bent, *A. canina*. All are suitable for turf formation. See Seed Mixtures.

COMMON BENT OR BROWN TOP *(A. tenuis)* A perennial with a tough blade capable of making fine turf and spreading by rhizomes or stolons. Slow to establish, shade tolerant, drought resistant and suitable for a wide range of soils – from sandy types to heavy clays. Present in most lawns and putting and bowling greens. Brown top flourishes throughout Europe and has also been established in Australia, New Zealand, North and South America and temperate Asia (Fig 3).

Some of the bred cultivars are:

'Bardot', fine-leaved, compact and of vivid green during the summer months; 'Tracenta', has fine narrow blades which maintain a good colour throughout summer; 'Highland', a fine-leaved variety but a little coarser than 'Tracenta', has good persistency and excellent winter colour, originates from the USA.

CREEPING BENT *(A. stolonifera)* A stoloniferous, tufted perennial capable of forming tightly knit, luxury type turf on light to medium alkaline soils of high nutrient levels. Creeping bent is a constituent of sea washed turf and found in most good quality lawns; it is however a very shy seeder and is often best used to produce turf by vegetative propagation (qv). Being stoloniferous, its leafy surface runners produce a matted turf, soft to tread and which can be akin in texture to a thick pile carpet. Games which rely on the ball to bounce can consequently not be played on turf made from creeping bent alone.

Also known as fiorin and white bent, it is widely distributed and found throughout Europe, North and South America, Australia, New Zealand and temperate Asia (Fig 4).

VELVET BENT *(A. canina)* A stoloniferous, tufted but short perennial of slower spreading habit than the similar red or creeping bent. It has fine leaves of somewhat soft growth. The seed is not always in plentiful supply (Fig 5).

A light green, velvety turf resistant to weed invasion can be grown from a cultivar named 'Novobent'. The turf is soft and springy and consequently unsuitable for ball games.

Benzene Hexachloride See BHC

17

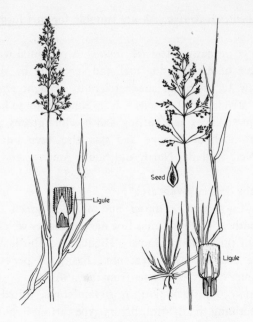

Fig 4 (left) Creeping Bent; Fig 5 (right) Velvet Bent

BHC

The commonly used abbreviation of a persistent organochlorine insecticide named benzene hexachloride. Effective against most insect pests including ants, chafer grubs and leatherjackets (qv).

BHC is available in both dust and liquid formulations; these vary in strength and individual manufacturers recommended application rates should always be observed. Liquids are more pleasant to use.

This material is dangerous to bees, fish and other livestock. It is also harmful to a number of ornamental and food plants.

Birds

Birds can be a nuisance on newly sown lawns, for by eating the seed they deplete the density of the sward. If seed pre-treated with a bird repellent is not being used, water the sown area with a liquid repellent such as Curb or Morkit.

Black cotton suspended from sticks and stretched 2-3in above the ground will keep birds at bay but is often impractical when large

18

areas are involved. Strips of tinfoil, old bottles painted red and inverted on a cane, or tin cans loosely suspended on a rope some two or three feet above ground are alternative means. Welcome starlings on mature turf as they come after leatherjackets (qv); similarly blackbirds and thrushes who will deplete the earthworm population and so save worm casts from spoiling the turf.

Bird's-foot Trefoil
Lotus corniculatus. A tap-rooted weed with bright yellow flowers, usually found on light sandy or limy soils. It has more than seventy common names, eg bacon-and-eggs and lady's slipper. Its long tap-root keeps the plant green during the driest summers. Applications of lawn sand repeated at monthly intervals, may help to eradicate this difficult and persistent weed. Alternatively slash the crowns with a sharp knife and sprinkle some ammonium sulphamate crystals on them; although a total weedkiller, it is unlikely to affect the rest of the lawn. See Weeds and Weedkillers and Appendix 3.

Black Medick
Medicago lupulina. A weed which flowers from early spring to late summer and produces fruits of black and twisted appearance. Fairly common and comparatively easily killed with mecoprop alone or mixed with 2,4-D. See Weeds and Weedkillers and Appendix 3.

Bonfire Ash
Often rich in potash, particularly where wood has been burnt. Although good for the garden in moderation, never apply it direct to fine turf as it may increase alkalinity.

Bordeaux Mixture
Now superseded for use on turf by more conveniently handled fungicides of greater efficiency. A messy mixture to prepare although it can be bought already mixed in powder form from some suppliers. A copper sulphate solution is combined with a hydrated lime suspension and both are passed through a strainer. The resultant mixture has to be used almost at once as it precipitates rather

quickly. If mixed with malachite green (qv), control of fusarium patch (qv) can be achieved. Only wooden or plastic containers can be employed as copper sulphate corrodes metals.

Brambles See Brushwood Killer and Appendix 3

Briars See Brushwood Killer and Appendix 3

Brown Patches
These can be caused by one or more of a number of factors. See under the following entries: Chafer Grubs, Dogs, Dollar Spot, Drought, Fusarium Patch, Leatherjackets, Petrol, Red Thread.

Brushing
Brushing turf can do nothing but good. It is a mild form of scarification, aerates the sward, removes small stones, worm casts and ant-hills, rids the grass of debris and makes it stand up better for the next cut with the mower. Use a besom or birch broom if possible and brush the lawn at least twice a year; spring and autumn. Top dressings (qv) should also be well brushed in.

Brushwood Killer
Several types are readily available which, when suitably diluted and applied, kill a broad spectrum of weeds including brambles, briars, trees, sucker growth, docks and bindweed. Materials of this kind are often useful when preparing neglected soils for turf purposes. As with all chemicals, carefully observe the manufacturer's instructions and pay special attention to the period of time which must elapse before treated ground can again be used for growing. Most brushwood killers contain 2,4,5-T alone or in combination with 2,4-D.
 See Weeds and Weedkillers and Appendix 3.

Bulbs Planting under turf; see Naturalising

Bumps and Hollows
Both flat and sloping lawns occasionally have slight imperfections due to faulty soil preparation or subsequent settlement. Bare patches soon develop on the highest spots as the mower will almost inevitably

scalp them. The lower areas are liable to be damp and hold water, the grass growing in them is longer and thicker and apart from looking unsightly, could encourage disease.

Provided that the differences in levels are not too great, application of top dressing (qv) can soon rectify the trouble, although several applications over a period of time may be necessary for complete success. Never apply too much top dressing at any one time; brush each dressing well into the turf and just permit the tips of the grass blades to show through. The grass may die if it is covered completely.

If the bumps and hollows are too severe, or if a more immediate cure is required, cut an H shape into the turf exactly above the rise or hollow. Carefully fold the turf back and either remove the excess soil or add some fresh; firm it well and replace the turf. The gaps created where the turf has been cut will knit together more quickly if a mixture of peat and sand is brushed well into them (Fig 6).

Buttercup

Two species are apt to invade turf: bulbous buttercup *(Ranunculus bulbosus)* which is without stolons and favours dry soils, and

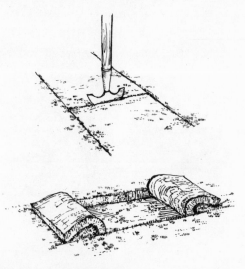

Fig   6 Correcting the level by rolling back, and
          adding or taking soil

creeping buttercup *(R. repens)* which, as the name would suggest, is stoloniferous and favours moist and heavy soils (Figs 7, 8). Both types respond to selective weedkillers listed in Appendix 3. See Weeds and Weedkillers.

Calomel
Mercurous chloride, a poison, used for the control of moss (qv) and fungal disease of turf.

Capsella bursa-pastoris See Shepherd's Purse

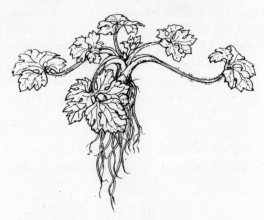

Fig 7 Bulbous Buttercup

Fig 8 Creeping Buttercup

Captan

A fungicide occasionally used as a seed dressing (qv) to control seedling diseases (qv). Apply 75 per cent Captan at the rate of 1oz per 28lb of seed.

Captan is a skin irritant with an unpleasant smell; also harmful to fish.

Carbaryl

An insecticide designed, among other things, for killing worms underground. Carbaryl is efficient, works quickly and eliminates the need for tiresome hand-sweeping of worms killed by other means.

Carefully observe instructions of use and recommended dosage rates given on the container label. Harmful to fish and dangerous to bees. See Earthworms.

Cat's-ear

Hypochaeris radicata. A perennial weed easily controlled with selective weedkillers in both new and mature lawns; do not permit it to grow uncontrolled for too long because its flat rosette of leaves smothers the grass below. See Appendix 3 for selective weedkiller recommendations; also Weeds and Weedkillers.

Cat's-tail

Phleum pratense, also known as Timothy-grass (qv).

Celandine, Lesser

Ranunculus ficaria. A tiresome weed that prefers moist and shady situations and multiplies by producing small bulbils (Fig 9).

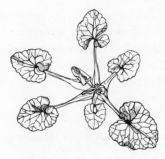

Fig 9 Celandine

23

Somewhat resistant to weedkiller but two applications, one month apart of either 2,4-D or MCPA can eradicate it. See Weeds and Weedkillers and Appendix 3.

Cerastium See Chickweeds

Chafer Grubs

These are the larvae or grubs of the May or June bug *(Melolontha melolontha)* or the garden chafer *(Phyllopertha horticola)*. The grubs live in the soil and are easily recognised by their dirty-white, fleshy and always curved bodies and milk chocolate coloured heads.

They feed on the roots of grass and cause bare patches or areas of withered grass. Grubs feed close to the surface during warm, humid spells in the autumn and spring and can be satisfactorily controlled at those times by watering the lawn with a BHC solution (qv) at the manufacturer's recommended application rate.

BHC is also effective against most other insect pests of lawns.

Chalk Soils See Soil Preparation

Chamomile

(Anthemis nobilis) see Grass Substitutes

Chemicals

When using any horticultural chemical please make sure that all the instructions on the label are carefully followed. See Appendix 2.

Chenopodium album See Fat Hen

Chewings Fescue See Fescues

Chickweeds

Cerastium species. A group of various species with spreading stems usually growing close to the ground. They favour most types of soil but can usually be controlled with one application of mecoprop. See Weeds and Weedkillers and Appendix 3.

Chlordane

A persistent organochlorine earthworm killer that also controls

24

leatherjackets and which should be used only when there is no other alternative.

When using, read and observe the instructions on the container label most carefully.

There are numerous alternative earthworm expellents and killers on the market. See Earthworms.

Chlorophyll
A green pigment present in plants; chlorophyll aids plants to manufacture carbohydrates from carbon dioxide and water, utilising energy from sunlight in the process of photosynthesis (qv).

Chloroxuron
A chemical used to control moss (qv).

Cinquefoil
Potentilla reptans. A common yellow-flowering perennial weed with a growth habit similar to a strawberry. Leaves consist of fine toothed leaflets carried on creeping stems which root. Responds to selective weedkillers. See Weeds and Weedkillers and Appendix 3.

Cirsium acaulon See Thistle

Cirsium arvense See Thistle

Clay Soils See Soil Preparation

Clover
Considered a weed if present in fine turf yet capable of producing a lawn if planted on its own. See Grass Substitutes.

Two of the many species of clover can however be tiresome weeds if growing in a fine-textured turf. White clover *(Trifolium repens)* and yellow suckling clover *(T. dubium)* are the two most usual and very easily recognised offenders. White clover can be killed with only one application of 2,4-D combined with either dichlorprop or fenoprop; yellow suckling clover requires at least two applications of the same mixture with one month interval between applications. See Weeds and Weedkillers and Appendix 3.

25

Coarse Grass

Patches of broad-leaved grasses can develop in fine turf; the grasses are either indigenous or the seed is brought in by birds or blown in. Regrettably there are no selective weedkillers that can eradicate coarse grass in lawns. If they are noticed when there are still only a few coarse leaves, the best way is to lever the turf up slightly with a garden fork and, provided the ground is moist, gently pull the leaves which normally come away quite cleanly, including the all important roots. Large patches are more tiresome to remove and slashing the coarse grass with a sharp knife, criss-cross fashion, is often advocated. Unfortunately it rarely does much good and with couch (qv) may cause more severe infestation. The only sure and satisfactory method is to dig out the whole of the offending patch; making certain all the roots are removed and refill with new soil, firm well and either re-seed or turf.

Cocksfoot

Dactylis glomerata. A tufted perennial more usefully employed as a constituent of grazing pastures than in turf production. Occasionally used for football pitches because of its deep rooting habit. Known as orchard-grass in the USA (Fig 10).

Common Bent

Agrostis tenuis also known as brown top. See Bent Grasses.

Compost

Compost is made from waste organic matter (fallen leaves, lawn mowings, fruit and vegetable peelings) which is stacked in a wire-net enclosure, trodden periodically for consolidation and kept for 12 months or so. Use a good compost activator and use it strictly according to manufacturer's instructions. When the compost is ready sift it through $\frac{1}{2}$in sieve and it makes a first class top dressing for the lawn.

Grass mowings from the first cut after weedkiller has been applied to the lawn should not be composted as weedkillers can remain active for several months.

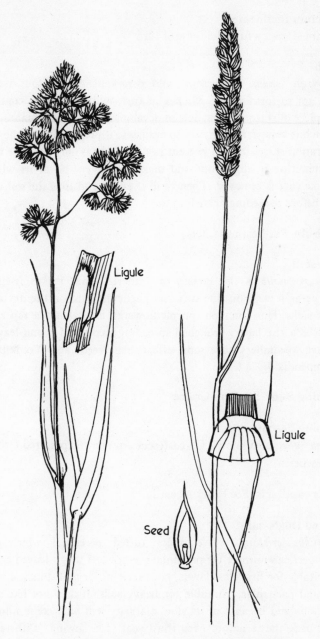

Fig 10 Cocksfoot   Fig 11 Crested Dog's-tail

Corticium fuciforme
Red thread (qv); a fungal disease of turf.

Couch
Agropyron repens. A tiresome and persistent rhizomatous weed-grass, apt to form coarse patches in turf, and difficult to control. Each piece of rhizome is capable of developing into a fresh plant.

Couch is comparatively easy to eradicate if present during the soil preparation stages (qv). If present in turf, there is only one sure way of eliminating it: dig it out and make sure every bit of its white, wire-like root is removed. Then refill the hole and firm the soil well down before re-seeding or turfing.

Crane-fly See Leatherjackets

Cranesbill
Geranium molle is the species of cranesbill that makes itself a nuisance as a weed on fine turf and particularly so on the dry and lighter soils. This common, purple-flowered annual has a tap root from which rise hairy, branched spreading stems and round leaves. Selective weedkillers have some effect. See Weeds and Weedkillers and Appendix 3.

Creeping Bent See Bent Grasses

Creeping Fescue
Festuca rubra also known as red fescue (qv) or creeping red fescue. See Fescues.

Crepis capillaris See Hawk's-beard

Crested Dog's-tail
Cynosurus cristatus. A compact tufted perennial which the non-expert can mistake for perennial rye-grass. A tough-leaved grass, not suitable for first class lawns, but excellent for withstanding hard wear and particularly suitable for heavy soils. It does not like acid conditions and because of its slow maturity will only come into its own during the second or even third year after sowing. Withstands drought and cold; retains its good colour (Fig 11).

Crowfoot

Ranunculus acris. A perennial weed also known as meadow buttercup and easily recognised as such. Typical yellow flowers and mostly found on moist soils. Susceptible to selective herbicides. See Weeds and Weedkillers and Appendix 3.

Culm

Another word for the hollow cylindrical and jointed stem of the grass plant.

Cultivar

A term for a species or hybrid variant maintained in cultivation by man. Gardeners frequently use 'variety' to describe such plants, but this should only refer to wild botanical forms. Only pre-1959 cultivar names may be in Latin form; from that date, new garden cultivars must have vernacular or fancy names.

A good example is *Lolium perenne* 'Melle'. *Lolium* is the genus, and *perenne* the species name of perennial rye-grass; 'Melle', the cultivar name is a bred plant of this. Cultivar is often shortened to cv.

Cumberland Turf See Turf Purchasing

Cynosurus cristatus See Crested Dog's-tail

Dactylis glomerata See Cocksfoot

Daffodils

Planting under turf; see Naturalising.

Daisy

Bellis perennis. A common perennial weed often found on lawns and easily recognised by its typical flower and rosettes usually growing close to the ground (Fig 12). Application of lawn sand can soon reduce their number and so can one or more applications of selective weedkiller. See Weeds and Weedkillers and Appendix 3.

Dalapon

A translocated herbicide which is very useful for the control of couch (qv) and other perennial as well as annual grasses. Because of this it

Fig 12 Daisy

must never be used on lawns but can be usefully employed during soil preparation (qv) and to kill grass on paths and drives.

Because Dalapon is not selective in use, extreme care must be exercised when using it among valuable crops. Dalapon is absorbed through leaves and roots and treated areas must not be planted for eight weeks after application. Never apply it during drought or frost; results are likely to be poor if rain falls within twelve hours of spraying.

Damping-off
A term used to describe the collapse of seedlings due to fungal infection. See Seedling Diseases.

Dandelion
Taraxacum officinale. A well-recognised perennial weed with taproots usually deeply anchored in the soil (Fig 13). Susceptible to selective weedkillers. See Weeds and Weedkillers and Appendix 3.

Fig 13 Dandelion

Derris
Useful as a worm killer if applied to turf during damp weather in spring and autumn. Various proprietary brands are readily available and application rates are dependent on the quantity of active ingredients present in individual formulations. Therefore read and follow the instructions on the label carefully. Derris can be applied both dry or wet but should be kept away from streams and ponds as the material is highly poisonous to fish. See Earthworms.

Deschampsia flexuosa See Wavy Hair-grass

Design
PURPOSE OF LAWN The lawn, large or small, is the foundation of the garden. It lends character, frames the house and extends the home. It accentuates the multi-coloured flower beds and other landscape features, it is the centrepiece of the garden and if well designed, adds spaciousness. The lawn may have to perform many duties – as a cricket pitch, a tennis court, for golf-putting practice, croquet and sun bathing. Only personal preference, combined with family needs and the natural advantages and limitations of both site and size can decide its use.

It is inevitable that lawns used for a variety of purposes suffer greater wear than those designed for ornamental use. But the children require a playground, the weekly wash must be hung out and if paths are not planned with care, visitors will always cut across the corner of the lawn instead of following the paths.

The use of new and purpose-bred grass cultivars combined with all the modern aids of lawn management mitigate the trouble, but there is unfortunately no real answer to hard and constant pounding of the living plants a lawn consists of – except one.

If space permits, make two lawns, perhaps separated by the house, a hedge or some other garden feature, one for play and utility purposes, the other more ornamental, to set off the plants. It may save a lot of heartache – for children and parents!

GARDEN PLANNING Whether a new garden is being made, or an existing one re-designed start by making a plan on paper. It is best to draw it to scale and to begin by marking the boundaries of the

31

property; then add the outlines of the house and other buildings. Remember also to indicate buildings and structures outside the boundaries which may need screening.

Paths are best sited along one or more sides of the turf. Avoid leading them directly on to the lawn, as the constant use of the same route soon wears bald patches in the sward; stepping stones sunk into the grass along the most travelled routes provide an interesting alternative.

Put the plan to the test before starting construction work. Place string or laths along the ground to outline the paths and other horizontal features of the garden. Indicate trees, shrubs and even planned-for structures by driving stakes of appropriate length into their proposed positions.

Now inspect the site from every possible view-point and angle, particularly from the various windows in the house. Does the proposed new willow hide ugly outbuildings from the dining room window? Is the site for the rose bed shaded by the proposed summerhouse? Is the compost heap out of sight? Ask every possible question, and only when every self-posed problem appears dealt with should construction start.

The less impatient gardener may prefer to start by making a lawn of the entire area – fence to fence lawn carpeting – and add the desired features over a period of time.

This also defers the not always insignificant financial outlay often necessary when stocking a virgin piece of ground. As familiarity with the house and its surroundings increases, new landscaping ideas are easily put into practice by digging out turfed areas of the required size, be they for flower border, rockery or even vegetable garden.

SIZE AND SHAPE Modern housing design and prevailing land prices are tending to decrease the size of gardens; but even a small area can assume spaciousness with careful planning. The more solid and unbroken the green expanse, the bigger it will seem.

The lawn can be any shape but the more it approximates a square or rectangle, the greater is the impression of space. Maximum impression of size is also gained by allowing the lawn to reach almost to the base of the house, dividing it only by a path or terrace. An uninterrupted expanse of turf is also much easier to construct and maintain. Most lawn operations are complicated and take longer if the lawn is irregularly shaped, has curved edges or if beds and trees are situated within the lawn area.

These hinder fertiliser and weedkiller applications and interfere with the sowing, rolling and mowing of the area. Permanent features are therefore best sited in a border lying between the garden boundary and lawn edges. Obstructions in the path of the mower must also be avoided if the regular pattern of alternate light and dark green stripes on your lawn is an aim. This pattern is produced by the rear roller of the mowing machine, and if its normal and straight course is diverted to cut around features let into the lawn, a pattern more akin to that of tracks at a railway junction results.

UNEVEN LAWNS Short cuts in gardening, particularly in lawn making, rarely succeed. An important exception is the sloping or undulating garden site. Take full advantage of such natural features as they reduce much of the tedious and laborious levelling needed for the proverbial 'billiard table' lawn and which is not necessarily always the most attractive. An inspection of any golf course confirms that the most beautiful greens are never completely flat and that their lie usually harmonises with the contours of the surrounding landscape.

Smooth and gentle undulations are preferable and should be in correct proportion to the overall area of the lawn. The larger lawn tolerates steeper inclines, whereas a smaller piece of grass with equally angled slopes looks ludicrous. Beware of undulations which are too sharp as the mowing machine will inevitably scalp the turf.

LAWN EDGES A first class lawn is only as neat as its edges; to keep them perfect can take longer than mowing the entire lawn, so keep them to the very minimum. See Edges.

GRASS BANKS AND VERGES Avoid grass banks if at all possible; they are difficult to establish and maintain. See Banks and Slopes.

Grass verges should be at least 30in wide; if narrower they lose their effectiveness and are difficult to mow. The heavier the traffic they have to bear, the wider they should be. See Soil Preparation, Drainage and Levelling.

Dichlorophen
A chemical used to control moss (qv) in turf.

Dichlorprop

A selective weedkiller usually obtainable combined with 2,4-D when it effectively controls a range of both annual and perennial weeds in mature turf. When used alone it controls a similar range of weeds as mecoprop and is particularly useful where knotgrass is a problem.

See Weeds and Weedkillers and also Appendix 3.

Digging

Digging is one of the basic gardening tasks and although it is considered fashionable to decry it, both soil and lawn-to-be will gain maximum benefit if preparatory work is carried out correctly.

Soil is dug (or mechanically turned with a plough or cultivator) to destroy weeds and to expose all large objects such as stones, rubbish and large roots which must then be removed. Even more important the surface is broken up so that air and moisture may penetrate to hasten the natural process which releases nutrients present in the soil. During digging, take the opportunity to add organic and other fertilisers and any soil conditioners that may be needed.

Single digging (ie one spade-blade length deep) should be adequate on most sites but if the job is to be done really well, fork the soil at the bottom of each trench.

To start, dig a trench the full width of the spade across one end of the plot to be dug and barrow the soil to the other end ready to fill the last trench. Facing the trench just exposed, start digging the next row by thrusting the blade of the spade to its full depth (approximately 10in) vertically into the soil. With the spade, lever the soil forward and then lift with the left-hand well down the spade's shaft. Then slightly lift the spade full of soil, aim it at the spot exactly opposite in the vacant trench and turn the blade through 180°. Repeat this along the whole of the row, spadeful after spadeful, until the end of the row when a whole new trench lies exposed.

Now fork the bottom of the trench to loosen the exposed soil before filling it with compost, manure or any other material designed to condition the soil before digging the next row.

Continue like this, row after row, always walking backwards away from the worked soil until the last trench at the end of the plot is exposed. Fill it with the soil previously dug from the first trench. If the soil is really heavy, it may be easier to use a fork instead of a spade, and if digging is carried out during the later part of winter or early spring, break each spadeful of soil into small pieces; but if digging is done during the autumn or early winter the frost and wet to come will perform this task.

See Soil Preparation.

Docks

Rumex species. A variable group of mostly perennial species occasionally found in turf as young and immature plants and at which stage they respond to selective herbicides. See Weeds and Weedkillers and Appendix 3.

Dogs

Dogs and cats often enjoy a romp on the lawn and rarely damage the turf. Bitch urine does however 'burn' the sward and causes brown patches surrounded by a ring of deep green grass. The grass on the affected spot eventually dies and coarse-leaved, weed grasses are apt to populate the area.

Unfortunately there is no satisfactory way of solving the problem except to keep bitches off the turf; in case of accidents, immediate flooding of the affected area with water may alleviate the damage.

Dollar Spot

Sclerotinia homoeocarpa. A fungal disease of turf which is easily recognised as it produces 2in diameter circular golden-brown coloured spots; these may develop and coalesce into large irregular shaped areas. Dollar spot is liable to attack during any time of the year but more usually during mild weather in late summer. It attacks bents and fescues as well as other grasses, red fescue being particularly susceptible. Provided infection is not severe an application of a fertiliser with high nitrogen content may assist the turf to recover.

Application of mercurous chloride (qv) offers some protection and control can be obtained with the very much safer fungicides quintozene and thiabendazole. All of them should be applied at makers' recommended rates.

Drainage

Adequate drainage is a necessity for good turf. Water-logged or very damp sites soon make themselves apparent by the invasion of moisture-loving sedges and mosses in the grass.

Drainage also improves the soil structure, aids the utilisation of plant foods, encourages plants to root deeply, and extends the growing season. Drained soils warm up earlier after the winter and retain their warmth longer in the autumn. Conversely, badly drained soils become greasy under wet conditions, and crack badly during periods of drought.

Drainage falls into two parts; the percolation of the water through the top six or nine inches of soil and further drainage through the sub soil so that the water penetrating the first layer can freely drain away. The particular requirements of a site can be determined by digging half a dozen 18-24in deep holes at intervals in the lawn area and watching them closely after heavy rain. If the water drains away and disappears completely within five or seven days, no further drainage system is necessary. If, however, the water level remains constant at about six to nine inches below soil level, some drainage must be undertaken. Nevertheless, this may not necessarily have to extend over the whole area. If the water lies only in certain of the tell-tale holes, a simply constructed soak-away or sump will cope with the excess.

A sump is simply made by digging a pit, 3-5ft deep and 3ft in diameter, where the surface water lies heaviest. Fill the bottom two thirds with large rubble or clinker. Follow this with a thick layer of smaller stones, topped off with a solid layer of ashes to make a firm bed for the top soil (Fig 14).

With such a sump all surplus water will gravitate into the pit and gradually disperse.

Fig 14 (left) Section of tile drain and (right) of soakaway

If the whole area requires draining only one drain is usually required for lawns up to tennis court size or even a little larger. This should be placed diagonally across the area in the direction of the natural fall. In extreme cases branch drains on the herringbone system can be added. With very large lawns the grid system is the more efficient, this comprises several drains running parallel, all of which enter a main drain. Whichever type of drain is used it must be given sufficient fall to carry off the water to the lowest point, there to discharge into a sump, ditch, pond or stream. Alternatively with a little ingenuity, it can be made to feed an ornamental water garden.

Drainage trenches should be wedge shaped, with firm bottoms, and sloping in the direction of the outlet at the rate of about 1 in 90. The depth of the trench is ruled by soil conditions, varying from 24in in heavy soils to 30in in light. Branch drains or laterals do not need to be quite as deep. They are usually 6in higher than the main drains they flow into. From 45° to 60° is the usual entry angle for the herringbone system, 90° for the grid system (Fig 15).

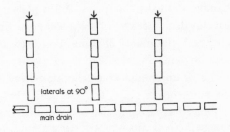

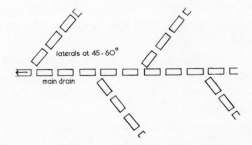

Fig 15 Grid and herring-bone drainage systems

The grid system in heavy clay necessitates drains at every 10-15ft, medium soils can afford a spacing of 20-30ft and in lighter soils, if indeed they need to be drained at all, up to 60ft should suffice. Having established that the system works by allowing water to flow along the freshly dug trenches to the outlet point, porous 12in long clay pipes must now be placed in position. A 4in diameter pipe will normally be sufficient for the main drain, with $2\frac{1}{2}$ or 3in for branch drains. Before the pipes are laid, all loose soil must be removed from the bottom of the trench. Then a 3in layer of clinker, coke or large coarse gravel is laid, on which the pipes are carefully aligned. A $\frac{1}{4}$in gap must be left between the pipes for the water to enter. Cover the pipes with another 3in layer of coarse clinker material, each particle of which must be noticeably bigger than the $\frac{1}{4}$in gap between pipes. Levelling off with a layer of fine gravel or ashes before finally replacing the soil, making certain that the top soil is uppermost. To avoid breakage of the pipes great care must be exercised when covering them with clinker. Remember they are made of clay and are brittle, like flower pots.

Slotted plastic pipes are more efficient and durable, and lighter and easier to handle, than the clay pipes. A 2in plastic pipe will do the work of a 3in clay drain because of its smoother surface.

With either method, the points of connection between drain and sump must always be piped, for blockage at this point will nullify the whole project. The drain should enter the soak-away at the point where the coarse stone layers cease, and the orifice be protected by large stones or rubble, decreasing in size with distance from it.

Another drainage method consists of placing a 6in layer of clinker over the whole area of the lawn underneath the top soil. The removal of the top soil on such a scale is, of course, a considerable task, and is perhaps only to be contemplated when it has to be done in any case for the purpose of levelling.

The 6in layer of clinker should be graded — large size first, then small and topped off with fine ashes. A similar clinker base can, if desired, be used to raise the lower levels of lawns to the same height as the remaining area.

See Soil Preparation and Levelling.

Drought See Watering

Earthworms

Important members of the soil fauna and valuable in gardens. They do however spoil lawns with the ugly casts of soil they bring onto the surface of the turf. Casts make all lawn operations more difficult and unless previously brushed away, are liable to be trodden on or flattened by the mower. This leaves a circular patch of bare consolidated soil ready for weed invasion; worse still in wet weather when casts cause slippery and muddy turf surfaces.

Dependent on the severity of the problem, it is always worthwhile to first try to remedy earthworm infestations with cultural methods before employing chemical controls.

Earthworms dislike water-logged conditions and are more likely to confine themselves to the lower regions of the soil if the water table is lowered by installing adequate drainage. Spiking and aeration also help, acid soils are also disliked by most species of earthworms. One of the best ways of achieving the correct level of acidity is to apply sulphate of ammonia or sulphate of iron (both constituents of lawn sand) and top dressings of peat. Also always remove grass mowings as these encourage earthworm activity.

Chemical control falls into two groups. Firstly those preparations that have to be applied every autumn and spring as they provide only temporary control; among them are mowrah meal, derris and permanganate of potash. All of these cause worms to rise to the surface and they then have to be swept up.

The second group includes more effective chemicals, chlordane and carbaryl, that provide long-term control up to three years and kill the worms in the soil. Both materials may also be effective against chafer grubs and leatherjackets present in the soil. Unlike the chemicals in the first group, carbaryl and chlordane are watered in.

Lead arsenate, which is a poison, is also a useful earthworm killer. Take great care when using it and keep children and pets away from treated areas for a minimum of six weeks after application.

All types of worm-killers are best applied to fresh mown turf during autumn or early spring. Choose a favourable period with the ground free from frost and the air temperature reasonably high.

However well the turf looks, its impression will be marred if the lawn edges are not kept well.

If the lawn is to be surrounded by concrete paths or a flagged terrace, make certain that the lawn level is fractionally higher so that the blades of the mower are not damaged by contact with the stone. If the lawn is to abut a gravel drive, build up the soil surface one or two inches above it, by using one of the modern plastic or metal lawn edgings, or thin board which has first been painted with a preservative. Flower beds adjoining the lawn or set in it, should have their edges similarly supported, particularly on light soils where they are apt to crumble during periods of dry weather. Neat, straight or curved edges, are simply constructed with an edging iron. This tool consists of a sharp half-moon shaped steel cutting blade fitted with a 3ft long handle.

Place a straight edge, or garden line, on the turf to guide the edging iron and press it into the sward to a depth of 2-3in in an outward slanting direction rather than directly vertical; the resulting ridge better supports the turf edge which is not as liable to crumble. Rock the edging iron, while still in the soil, slightly to the left and right, before withdrawing it. Allow the second cut to overlap the first slightly and continue along the whole edge in a similar manner. Established edges require little maintenance apart from being trimmed after the first spring mowing. After each subsequent cut, the overlapping grass is best cut with shears or one of the powered edge trimmers, as too frequent use of the edging iron gradually decreases the lawn area (Fig 16).

Creosote kills grass and a two or three inch wide strip painted along a turf edge slightly below the surface of an abutting terrace or path saves a lot of difficult and time-consuming work with the edge-clippers. The soil acting herbicide simazine (qv) also kills grass and may be used for the same purpose. Apply these materials carefully or the lawn edge is likely to be ragged. Broken edges can be repaired by cutting and lifting the section of turf with the broken part. Turn the turf round so that the bad edge faces into the lawn. Fill the hole with fresh soil, firm and re-seed.

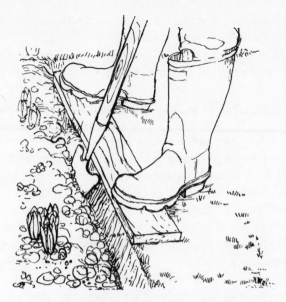

Fig 16 Trimming edges with a turfing iron

Epsom Salts

Magnesium sulphate. This provides a temporary control for fairy rings (qv); dissolve 2oz in 1gall of water and apply this mixture to every sq yd of diseased turf.

Erodium cicutarium See Storksbill

Fairy Rings

The fairy ring fungus (*Marasmius oreades* and others), starts with a small group of fungi and spreads gradually outwards into a big ring. Sometimes, and especially during the summer, the ring is composed of three separate zones or rings, two of dark green healthy grass and a central one between them where the turf is wilted, brown and often dead.

These contrasting conditions are brought about by the ability of the fungus to produce ammonia salts which bacteria change into nitrates. This temporarily enriches the grass making it grow lushly and dark green. Grass in the inner circle may die or brown off as a

41

result of drought caused by the fungal threads (mycelium) forming a waxy and waterproof mat in the soil.

The fairy ring fungus seems to attack most species of grass and if present, symptoms can usually be found during most mild periods of the year.

This disease is difficult to control because the mycelium can be as deep as 18in in some soils and its waxy nature makes it virtually impossible for water and chemicals to penetrate and effect a cure.

The first rule is always to collect all fungi as soon as they appear and to destroy them. If the disease can be tackled soon after it first appears, adequate control may be achieved by spiking the affected area to a depth of 4-6in and drenching each square yard of turf with a solution of 2oz of sulphate of iron in $\frac{1}{2}$gall of water. Epsom Salts have also been recommended for this purpose at 2oz per 1gall of water applied per sq yd.

In cases where the disease is more firmly established it is often necessary to strip the turf not only from the affected area but including at least a 2ft wide margin of surrounding grass. Remove the turf carefully and do not permit it to contaminate clean ground. Fork the exposed area and apply formaldehyde (qv) which is a poison. (For every 10sq yd to be treated, well stir 6pt of 40 per cent formaldehyde and $\frac{1}{2}$pt of wetting agent into 10gall of water). To retain the fumes, cover the area with sacks or polythene for a period of 7-10 days. After removal of the covers, fork the soil again to permit all fumes to escape but allow at least six weeks to elapse before making up the soil level and re-seeding or turfing. To minimise the risk of spreading the disease to other areas of the garden, tools used during this operation should be washed in the formaldehyde solution before they are used for other work.

Another method, but without the aid of chemical preparations, is to dig the rings out to a depth of at least 12-18in and replace with fresh soil.

Fat Hen
Chenopodium album can be a common weed on cultivated ground. Often found on newly sown lawns but causes no damage and is soon mown out.

Fenoprop

Belongs to the same group as mecroprop; both are selective weedkillers and capable of controlling both annual and perennial weeds in mature turf. Fenoprop is even more effective if combined with 2,4-D and proprietary mixtures are available under a number of different brand names.

See Weeds and Weedkillers and also Appendix 3.

Fertilisers and Feeding

To keep established lawns in good condition, regular feeding is a necessity. Grass growth, constantly cut and removed, exhausts plant foods which must be replenished if the sward is to remain of good colour, healthy and vigorous.

Turf needs three essential elements: nitrogen (N) to encourage leaf development; phosphate (P) to assist root growth so essential for the plants to be able to take up their full share of moisture and nutrients; and potash (K) to provide the sward with a healthy constitution and increase disease resistance. See Nitrogen, Phosphate and Potash.

The inherent nutrient content of soils varies widely and is apt to fluctuate according to soil type, its situation and previous cropping. The only reliable way to assess the correct amount of the various plant foods required by your lawn is to use one of the inexpensive and readily available soil testing kits. Their use rapidly decides the problem. All that is necessary is to collect small amounts of soil from the lawn area, mix them with the chemicals supplied in the kit and depending on the reaction of the mixture, read the answer from the chart supplied. This provides a tailor-made formula of the type and amounts of fertiliser your lawn needs at that particular time. The initial cost of the kit is soon saved by reduced expenditure on excess fertiliser applications which may otherwise be made.

PROPRIETARY FERTILISERS Many proprietary makes of lawn fertiliser containing nitrogen, phosphorus and potassium in ready mixed and correctly balanced form, are readily available and if used in accordance with the manufacturer's instructions, give very good results under most conditions. Use one containing approximately 10 per cent nitrogen, 5 per cent phosphate and 3 per cent potash. Some formulations also incorporate weedkiller. If you prefer to compound your own fertiliser, the cost is less and good results are obtained with a mixture of $\frac{1}{2}$oz sulphate of ammonia, 1oz superphosphate and $\frac{1}{4}$oz sulphate of potash. Purchase a sufficient quantity of each so that this amount can be applied to every square yard of lawn area. The three materials are easily mixed in the bottom of a wheel-barrow with either trowel or spade and should be bulked up with four or five times their weight of sand and soil.

Use the mixture soon after making it or it is apt to cake and form lumps. Its keeping properties can be increased by adding organic fertiliser in the form of $\frac{1}{2}$oz finely ground bonemeal (mostly phosphatic) and an equally fine $\frac{1}{2}$oz hoof and horn meal (contains slowly releasing nitrogen) and applying the resulting mixture at the rate of 2oz per sq yd.

WHEN TO APPLY FERTILISER Grasses, with their comparatively shallow root system, need small quantities of fertiliser at regular intervals throughout the growing season – let a 'little and often' be the rule. For maximum benefit applications must commence during early spring to encourage the finer grasses, which start their growth cycle earlier in the season then their coarser-leaved growing neighbours, and which are therefore unable to take full advantage of the freshly supplied plant food so early in the season.

Continued applications of NPK fertiliser should follow at four to six weekly intervals right through the growing season to just past mid-summer. Drop the nitrogen from the dressing then or the turf becomes over stimulated and its lush and soft growth so late in the year increases disease risk and inability to withstand satisfactorily the cold of the autumn and winter months. Instead place the emphasis on a phosphate/potash dressing for the last application of the year. This should take place during the late autumn and helps to increase disease resistance and root development which in turn get the lawn off to a good start during the following spring.

For home produced fertiliser mixture nitrogen should be excluded from the formula; if proprietary makes are bought, special autumn/winter formulations are available to achieve the same results.

Soil analysis, or the poor colour of the grass, may indicate that only nitrogen applications are required during the summer months.

In this case $\frac{1}{2}$oz of sulphate of ammonia dissolved in $\frac{1}{2}$gal of water and applied to every square yard, is all that is necessary. If you prefer to apply sulphate of ammonia in dry form, never use it neat, but mix it with a carrier of finely sifted compost at the rate 4oz per sq yd. Sulphate of ammonia is very apt to scorch lawns and must be used most carefully.

New and ever improved fertilisers are continually coming on the market; one of the more recent improvements is a fertiliser that releases nitrogen rather more slowly than other forms and often only one early spring application, instead of the normal two or three dressings over the season is sufficient.

The later in the growing season this type of fertiliser is used, the smaller must be the amount applied to avoid the over stimulation of grasses through the presence of excess nitrogen late in the growing year. Manufacturer's instructions take care of this and should be carefully observed.

HOW TO APPLY FERTILISERS It is essential to achieve even and proper distribution of fertiliser. If sections are missed, however small, they look weak and anaemic at the side of the fed turf. Similar contrasts also arise when some patches of the ground receive more than their normal dose.

The safest method is to mark the area out with string first or to use a template as with the sowing of grass seed. Another precaution is to divide the bulk to be applied into two equal halves, and spread each half in opposite directions. All these points apply to both liquid and dry formulations.

A mechanical distributor (see Lawn Spreader) is, of course, the most fool-proof method, but even then care must be used to avoid overlapping, or excessive application on turning the machine. The wheel tracks of the distributor on the grass surface provide a good guide and turning can be avoided by bodily lifting the machine when the lawn edge is reached. (A 14in wide distributor filled with fertiliser weighs little more than 14lb).

WHEN NOT TO APPLY FERTILISER Never apply fertiliser dressings immediately before mowing, or a portion of the application is carried off with the grass clippings; give the fertiliser a chance to work in, or if rain does not follow within two days, give the lawn a good soaking.

Fertilisers, especially sulphate of ammonia, must never be applied during periods of drought when they are apt to scorch the grass without providing any benefit. For maximum results, the grass should be dry when the mixture is applied, but the soil moist.

Ferrous Sulphate See Sulphate of Iron

Fescues A genus of dwarf growing grasses with fine, bristle-like leaves presenting the best choice for making first grade ornamental lawns in combination with bents (qv) and under specialised conditions, also meadow-grass (qv).

CHEWINGS FESCUE (*Festuca rubra commutata*) A tufted perennial with rhizomes capable of producing fine turf. Drought resistant and therefore suitable for sowing on the lighter and drier soils. Does not do well on cold, heavy clay soils. Normally dark green in colour but some strains seem to discolour just below the mower cut on the leaf tip (Fig 17).

When sowing bent grasses in combination with Chewings fescue it is advisable to sow a bigger proportion of fescue as the aggressive bents provide severe competition. The unusual name of this grass derives from Mr Chewings who first sold the seed in New Zealand and subsequently exported large quantities to England. Chewings fescue is now widely used throughout Europe, North America and, of course, New Zealand.

Some of the available cultivars are: 'Barfalla' – non-rhizomatous, good tillering and consequently able to form close turf; 'Flevo' – fine-leaved, withstands close mowing, fair tolerance to hard wear; 'Highlight' – perhaps the best existing cultivar of Chewings fescue, covers the ground well, good winter colour and equally attractive during growing season; 'Koket' – dark green during the summer, fine leaves, tolerates drought conditions; 'Waldorf' – better colour than 'Highlight' during the summer and shows resistance to red thread disease (qv).

FINE-LEAVED SHEEP'S FESCUE (*Festuca tenuifolia*) Fine-leaved tufted perennial capable of forming close turf. Remains dark green, tolerates shady conditions and dry and acid soils. Not recommended as a constituent for grass seed mixtures intended for fine turf, but

Fig 17 (left) Chewings Fescue; Fig 18 (right) Fine-leaved Sheep's Fescue

ideal for special situations that exploit its qualities, eg woodlands (Fig 18). It is known as hair fescue in the USA.

HARD FESCUE *(Festuca longifolia)* A non-rhizomatous, tufted perennial which was at one time used in mixtures for the establishment of grass-land but is now comparatively rare; there are many better grasses available today. Occasionally confused with sheep's fescue which is superior (Fig 19).

'Biljart' is a cultivar only suitable for ornamental lawns because of its inability to withstand hard wear. It keeps its dark green colour throughout summer and winter and shows some resistance to red thread disease (qv). Good shade tolerance and drought resistance.

RED FESCUE, CREEPING FESCUE *(Festuca rubra)* A rhizomatous perennial with numerous variants, each possessing different

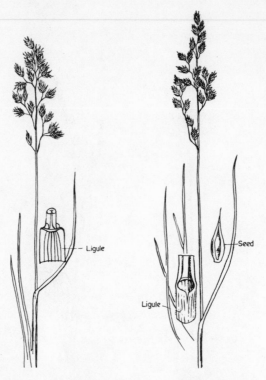

Fig 19 (left) Hard Fescue; Fig 20 (right) Red Fescue

characteristics, used for the production of fine quality turf. A fine-bladed grass able to establish close, springy turf on a wide range of soils excepting heavy clay (Fig 20).

A fair number of good cultivars are available, some of which are: 'Aberystwyth S59' – gives good performance under close mowing, blends well with bents; 'Dawson' – a strain from the Sports Turf Research Institute (qv) at Bingley, Yorkshire, England, fine-leaved but apt to loose its normally good colour during winter; 'Golfrood' – bred in Holland, it is similar to the red fescue found in Cumberland marsh turf (qv), it spreads well, extremely fine leaf, apt to discolour during spring frosts and susceptible to dollar spot disease (qv); 'Novorubra' – a versatile, rhizomatous cultivar with persistency; 'Oasis' – distinctive light green colour, prone to yellowing during the winter months.

Ligule

Fig 21 Sheep's Fescue

SHEEP'S FESCUE *(Festuca ovina)* A perennial grass, without rhizomes, rather tufted. Drought resistant, winter hardy and tolerant of close cutting. Occasionally confused with hard fescue which is inferior. Seed from sheep's fescue is often difficult to obtain (Fig 21). A cultivar known as 'Novina' is said to have finer and darker coloured leaves than commercial types.

Festuca species See under Fescues

Field Wood-rush
Luzula campestris looks like a broad-leaved grass which invades turf but can be controlled with mecoprop. See Weeds and Weedkillers and Appendix 3.

Fine-leaved Sheep's Fescue *Festuca tenuifolia* see Fescues

Fiorin
A name for creeping bent. See Bent Grasses.

49

Foliar Feeding

Turf is normally fed by applying nutrients in dry or liquid forms which the grass takes up through its roots. Manufacturers are now supplying foliar fertilisers that are taken up through the leaf. An ideal method for many plants but not so very satisfactory for grass. Grasses have a comparatively small leaf area and the finer the grass, the smaller the leaf area, eg fescues and bents. The broader-leaved and more undesirable grasses are therefore able to take up greater quantities of liquid feed and consequently predominate in the sward.

Foliar feeds can also be combined with weedkillers but manufacturers' advice should be sought to make sure that the chosen compounds are compatible.

Formaldehyde

A chemical which in Britain is subject to the Poisons Act and used as a soil sterilant. Several grades are available but the 40 per cent formaldehyde concentration is the most frequently used. A useful material for the control of fairy rings (qv). Treated soils should not be replanted until all fumes and smell have disappeared; this usually takes six weeks but somewhat less on the really light soils.

Fungi

Various types may appear sporadically on lawns, especially during wet, humid periods in the autumn. These are not necessarily the first signs of fairy rings (qv) but usually arise from rotting organic matter in the soil such as tree roots.

Elimination by chemical means is not always successful and if fungi persist and are spoiling good turf it may be advisable to excavate the source of trouble. To prevent spores from spreading always gather the fungi as soon as they appear and destroy them.

Other controls may be tried and perhaps the most convenient is mercurised turf fungicide normally used for the control of moss. An alternative is Epsom Salts applied after first spiking the ground, at 2oz per gal of water per sq yd.

Fungicide

A chemical for controlling fungi. Specific recommendations are given under the names of the particular diseases.

Fusarium See Seedling Diseases (qv)

Fusarium nivale
A fungal disease of turf also known as fusarium patch (qv) and snow mould.

Fusarium Patch
Also known as snow mould and one of the most common diseases attacking turf; caused by the fungus *Fusarium nivale*. The disease is more prevelant during mild spells occurring between autumn and early spring although attacks, which can occur quite suddenly, are also possible when cool and humid conditions coincide with an overcast sky during the summer. Fusarium often follows a thaw of snow with outbreaks occurring in the very spots where the lawn has been trodden on when covered with snow.

At first, fusarium causes small, yellow-brown, almost circular patches, two or three inches in diameter, these enlarge rapidly until several affected areas from 12-18in across coalesce. Occasionally, and mostly during wet weather, pink or white cotton-wool like fungus appears on the diseased areas.

Annual meadow-grass is usually severely affected by fusarium whilst some other grasses like red fescue, although susceptible, suffer less severely. Crested dog's-tail, perennial rye-grass and smooth-stalked meadow-grass are said to be resistant.

Avoid applying lime, as this increases the risk of fusarium attacks. So also will fertiliser containing nitrogen applied after mid-summer. Keep the turf firm, well mown and aerated.

Less severe attacks may be checked temporarily with a solution of 1oz of sulphate of iron in 2gal of water sprayed through a fine rose or sprinkle bar over 4sq yds. For more effective and permanent control apply mercurised lawn sand at 4oz per sq yd. Other useful fungicides are quintozene and thiabendazole. Always treat the whole of the area, not just the affected patches.

In the case of fusarium, chemicals are best used in an endeavour to prevent attacks rather than to cure them after they have occurred. Apply the first dose during the autumn and repeat at monthly intervals while conditions favour fungal attack.

Galium saxatile See Heath Bedstraw

Geranium molle See Cranesbill

Germination

The development from seed of a plant complete with shoots and roots. Usually expressed, after laboratory tests, as the percentage of pure named seeds that are viable. Never buy grass seeds of less than 90 per cent germination.

Glaux maritima See Sea Milkwort

Gorse See Brushwood Killers and Appendix 3

Grain See Matted Turf

Grass Breeding

The main aim of plant breeding is to improve existing plants in one or more respects. Flowers are perhaps the best example, where breeding not only improves the colour of blooms but also their size and number as compared with the same species in the wild. The plant breeder's work on grasses is just as effective and dramatic although somewhat less apparent to the layman, unless individual members of the same grass species are studied closely and compared side by side.

The turf enthusiast only rarely sees the whole grass plant complete with stem and flowering head; he only sees grass in the form of turf when plants are in a constantly defoliated state. But the breeder has to study the whole plant and make many crosses and selections over a number of years to perfect useful new cultivars.

Prior to emphasis being placed on specifically breeding grasses for turf production, the only readily available types were often those that yielded the largest quantities of seed and were consequently the cheapest to produce. It is this type of seed which is known as commercial seed; it is seed of doubtful origin and not necessarily the ideal for the production of good quality turf.

The breeding of new turf-grass cultivars started somewhat later than breeding for the more important food and ornamental species. Many grass species, including a wide range of variants within species, are available to the breeder who has to disregard the criterion of high seed yields and concentrate on breeding cultivars that combine as many as possible of the qualities desirable for the production of turf. The cost of the new grass cultivars would, of course, have to reflect their possible, though not inevitable, lower seed bearing capacity; but against this doubtful and only marginal cost increase, new cultivars provide numerous advantages. Some of these are:

improved germination, seedling vigour and high level of establishment; better growth and rapid recovery after heavy wear and constant mowing; good colour persisting throughout the year; resistance to diseases, drought, hard wear and winter conditions including frost; density of the sward and persistency; height, longevity and habit of growth.

Breeders aim to combine the maximum number of good characteristics within the same cultivar; this takes many years of work and ever better cultivars are continually reaching the market. Several of them are mentioned and described under the relevant species; but their number and continual increase makes it impossible to make cultivar lists exhaustive.

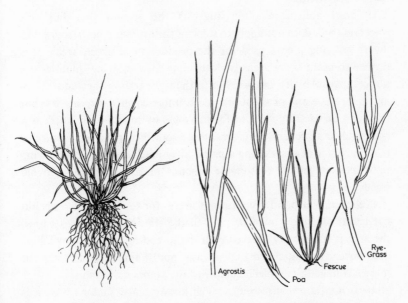

Fig 22 (left) Grass plant; Fig 23 (right) Different types of grass leaf

53

RECOGNITION OF BRED GRASSES Bred cultivars are usually given a name to distinguish them from other cultivars. *Poa pratensis* 'Monopoly' is the full name of a cultivar of smooth-stalked meadow-grass. *Poa* is the genus name and *pratensis* the species name and which in combination *(Poa pratensis)* form the specific name. The cultivar name, in this case 'Monopoly', is always added at the end.

Grass Plant

The roots of grasses are mostly fibrous, without tap roots, and have the ability to recover quickly and regenerate after mechanical damage (Fig 22). This characteristic is turned to good advantage when scarifying or spiking turf. See Aeration.

Grasses are best distinguished by the shape of their leaves and examination of ligules, clearly illustrated in the case of all important turf-grasses (Fig 23). Additional basic differences can also be observed in their flower heads which the turf enthusiast only rarely sees!

Grass Substitutes

The word substitute often suggests the second best but this interpretation does not apply to some of the aromatic herbs and other dwarf growing plants used for the production of green areas. It is unwise to plant large areas with them as their wearing qualities are not comparable with grasses, but in the right setting they add charm and interest. None of them provide suitable cover for sports use but they can be usefully sited to form a mass of colour on a bank, as a surround to a rockery or to accentuate some other garden feature or take the place of grass along a path. They need less frequent mowing than grasses, but a reasonable amount of management to avoid weeds.

Preliminary ground preparations are as for sowing grass seeds but particular attention must be paid to the elimination of weeds until the area is completely covered with the spreading plants. Weedkillers used for conventional grass lawns must not be applied at any stage or severe damage or complete collapse of the plants may result.

CHAMOMILE *(Anthemis nobilis)* Well known since Tudor times, it is undoubtedly the best known and most frequently used grass

54

substitute. It has prostrate running stems, with feathery, deep green aromatic foliage. Chamomile grows well on nearly all types of soil, with the exception of heavy clay, and produces a springy turf that stands up well to drought. Chamomile seed (80,000 seeds per oz) is particularly small and is sown like grass seed, at the rate of 1/16 oz per sq yd. Even distribution of this small quantity is facilitated by mixing the seed with four or five times its own bulk of fine silver sand and sowing it with an old sugar castor or through a fine sieve.

An alternative is to raise seedlings for transplanting. During early spring, sow the seed in boxes which have previously been filled with a good proprietary brand of seed-raising compost. Distribute the seeds thinly and as evenly as possible and cover them with just a sprinkling of compost before firming lightly. Place the boxes out of doors, preferably in a sheltered position, keep moist but protect from heavy rain. When the plants are sufficiently large enough to handle, usually during the early summer, plant them out on the lawn area from three to six inches apart. The closer the spacing between plants the more rapidly they join and close over the bare ground. Keep the area weeded and mow for the first time with cutting blades set high, soon after the plants are established in their new quarters and certainly before they meet in the rows. Mowing encourages lateral spread and keeps flowerheads away.

Always mow regularly and never allow the plants to flower, as this dissipates their energy and they are apt to grow in a straggly manner instead of forming compact turf. An annual top dressing of a good lawn compost applied during the autumn at the rate of 1-2lb per sq yd is beneficial. Plants can be bought from specialist nurseries.

CLOVER One of the best known plants and admirably suitable for lawn making. It is more drought resistant than chamomile or thyme and remains green even when grasses flag from moisture shortage. Wild white clover *(Trifolium repens)* is a persistent wild form which spreads very close to the ground and the best type for making a lawn. Preferably sown during spring, it is distributed like grass seed at the rate $\frac{3}{4}$-$1\frac{1}{4}$oz per sq yd. Unlike grass, clover likes alkaline conditions and grows well over a wide range of soils. It needs less cutting than normal turf but fairly regular mowing keeps the clover leaves small and prevents flowering.

Bee keepers need mow even less frequently as the flowers, produced on barely 6in high stems, are valuable for bees to turn into delicious honey. Swards made from clover are deep green, dense, hard wearing and smother weeds but suffer from the disadvantage of being slippery when wet.

PEARLWORT *(Sagina species)* Usually considered a pernicious weed in fine turf, but if raised from seed and planted out like chamomile it makes a rich green and dense sward. It is used in the drier parts of France and Italy for just that purpose. *S. subulata* and *S. glabra* are the best species for lawn making and should be sown during spring on light soils in sunny situations. Weeds, especially perennials, can be troublesome and unless carefully removed are liable to swamp the lawn. Mowing, with cutting blades set high, must be carried out frequently, and rolling is beneficial.

PENNYROYAL *(Mentha pulegium)* An aromatic herb exuding a strong peppermint scent. It is deep green and capable of producing a thick sward which needs little cutting. Pennyroyal has a preference for light soils and dislikes shade. Like chamomile it can be sown direct during the spring, or raised from seedlings for subsequent planting out at 6in intervals.

THYME *(Thymus species)* Capable of making a sweet scented and colourful sward particularly if a mixture of several cultivars, all producing different coloured flowers, are judiciously planted. Raise the plants from seed sown during early spring and plant out at 4-6in spacings. If areas of different colours are wanted, there are many fine cultivars available, and to obtain maximum effect they should be planted in carefully arranged groups of four, five or six of the same colour.

Thyme turf may be walked upon but not too frequently. Apart from trimming off the spent flower heads with either mower or shears, little cutting is required, and one annual top dressing at the end of the growing season is all the attention needed.

The most acceptable cultivars for a wide range of soils, except the heaviest clays, are many and some are listed here, all are derived from *T. serpyllum* which is prostrate in growth habit. All are aromatic and scent and foliage are only mentioned if they differ from the normal.

	Foliage	Flower
'Alba'		White
'Annie Hall'	Dark Green	Pale Pink
'Coccineus'	Dark Green	Red
'Lanuginosus'	Silver-grey	Heather Purple
'Pink Chintz'		Salmon

Green Vitriol See Sulphate of Iron

Groundsel
Senecio vulgaris is a harmless weed often found in gardens and also on newly sown lawns. It causes little damage and soon disappears as a result of regular mowing.

Growth Regulator
A chemical capable of retarding growth. Products of this nature should never be used on fine turf but are useful to slow down the normal growth rate of grass on ground where mowing is difficult, expensive or undesirable, eg some amenity areas, roadside verges, cemeteries, slopes and steep banks, industrial sites, paddocks and waste ground.

Several proprietary brands are available some of which can be mixed with 2,4-D (qv) to improve control of broad-leaved weeds; all should be used strictly in accordance with maker's instructions.

Retardants can be expected to suppress the growth of grass for 8-10 weeks and are normally applied during the spring when grass is 4-6in high and actively growing.

Gypsum
An excellent conditioner for heavy and sticky soils, also known as sulphate of lime. Contrary to popular belief, gypsum does not influence the pH (qv) of soils and can be used liberally to improve the structure of soils intended for turf. Fork 6-8oz per sq yd into the top 4-6in of the ground unless the soil is particularly heavy, when the application rate may be doubled.

Hair Fescue
A name for fine-leaved sheep's fescue; see Fescues.

Hard Fescue See Fescues

Hawk's-beard
Crepis capillaris. A tap rooted, narrow-leaved, erect weed with small yellow dandelion-like flowers. A single application of either MCPA or 2,4-D usually controls this weed. See Weeds and Weedkillers and Appendix 3.

Hawkbit
Two species can be found in lawns, both are perennial weeds. The first is known as autumn hawkbit *(Leontodon autumnalis)* and is without the hairs on the leaves which chiefly distinguish it from the hairy common hawkbit *(L. hispidus)*. Both are satisfactorily controlled with selective herbicides. See Weeds and Weedkillers and Appendix 3.

Heath Bedstraw
Galium saxatile. A perennial weed with small white flowers and procumbent stems which bear narrow leaves in whorls of four to six. Usually only present where soils are somewhat acid. Succumbs, when treated with one or more applications of selective herbicide. See Weeds and Weedkillers and Appendix 3.

Helminthosporium See Seedling Diseases

Herbicide
A chemical preparation for killing weeds. See Weeds and Weedkillers.

Holcus lanatus See Yorkshire Fog

Hollow Tine Fork See Aeration

Hypochaeris radicata See Cat's-ear

Indigenous
Belonging naturally to an area, ie a plant which has not been introduced.

Insecticide
A chemical which kills insects.

Internode
The portion of stem between two nodes.

Ioxynil
A selective weedkiller which can be applied to newly sown turf but not before the grasses have reached the two-leaf stage. Ioxynil, available under a variety of trade names, controls seedling weeds which so often germinate at about the same time as the grasses in freshly sown lawns.

Combinations of ioxynil and mecoprop are also available and are particularly effective against the otherwise difficult to control speedwells. See Weeds and Weedkillers and also Appendix 3.

Kentucky Blue-grass
The name used in N America for smooth-stalked meadow-grass. See Meadow-grasses.

Knotgrass
Polygonum aviculare. An annual weed also known as knotweed. Its long wiry stems, carrying small red flowers, quickly colonise ground and will not yield to mecoprop. Two successive applications of MCPA or 2,4-D timed with a one month interval between them should show results. See Weeds and Weedkillers and Appendix 3.

Lady's Slipper See Bird's-foot Trefoil

Lamium purpureum See Nettles

Lawn Making
Lawns can be made from turf, seed or, more rarely, by planting grass roots (for the last, see Planting a Lawn). All three methods produce satisfactory sward but the final choice depends on careful consideration of their respective merits and disadvantages as applied to the site.

SEED Although seed sown during spring or autumn provides a green cover within weeks, it takes a year or two before thick, springy and verdant turf is formed. Naturally the young grass will stand a certain amount of wear and tear but if fine turf is wanted, care and patience are necessary to nurse it during its early life.

Grass seed is usually supplied in the form of a mixture of different grasses which have been most carefully blended to suit differing types of soil and use. Always buy the mixture to suit the purpose and never purchase cheap grass seed; this is certainly false economy and produces unsuitable turf of poor quality. Select a good seed supplier, an expert in his field and whose judgment you can trust. He will always be pleased to make up a special grass mixture to suit your particular requirements.

Grass seed prices vary a little from season to season, depending on previous harvests and world supply. When buying grasses, it is useful to remember that the poorer grasses, with broad leaves and thick stems, are the prolific producers of usually the biggest seeds; the slower-growing, fine-leaved and thin-stemmed grasses have smaller seeds and are more expensive. For this reason a mixture intended to produce a leafy, hard wearing play area is always cheaper than one for the production of fine compact turf. See Seed Mixtures, Soil Preparation and Sowing.

TURF The use of turf is undoubtedly the most expensive method of producing a lawn but provides a compact and ready to use sward a few weeks after laying. The work is best undertaken during autumn or winter so that there is plenty of moisture for the grass roots to grow into.

If the lawn is being laid on very heavy clay it is easier to turf than to prepare the very much finer tilth needed for seed sowing. Turfing does, however, present the gardener with a dilemma and entices the impatient and unwary to stint the preparatory ground work in the false hope that the turves will cover any neglect. They may do so for a little while but after a few months, weeds will push through, and turves sink to the contour of the insufficiently prepared ground below.

Turf is best bought from a nursery which specialises in this type of work. There are not many of them and it will certainly be more expensive than that obtained from an old meadow. Meadows, usually broken up by farmers for sale to gardeners may only be worn out agricultural grazing land. The best attention it is ever likely to have had is grazing by animals and the odd spray of weedkiller. Turf from some building sites may well be in better condition and perhaps be cut from an old lawn of an existing house.

Visit the site and examine the turf before you finally order. Good turf is weed free and of good colour; it has an even texture and contains no coarse grasses. Turves are sold ready cut, usually 3ft long by 1ft wide and vary in thickness from one to two inches. If too thin they will dry out quickly and rapidly deteriorate if they are not immediately laid on arrival at site; if excessively thick, transport costs will be increased disproportionately.

Cumberland and sea marsh turf are as excellent as their reputation, but best avoided for ordinary lawn purposes. They grow well on the rich black soils from which they stem but it is almost impossible to keep them in their original fine state when they are transplanted to soil and climatic conditions quite alien to their natural habitat. Fine turf of this nature is best suited to golf and bowling greens where the simulation of its native environment combined with daily attention, prevents it from degenerating too rapidly. Turf of this kind is even more highly priced, and unless you happen to live near its source, transport is inordinately dear. See Turfing.

OTHER METHODS Ready-to-lay lawn carpets are now available. They consist of two layers of fibrous paper-like material containing the already correctly spaced seed. The material is purchased in the form of rolls of varying widths, and spread over the soil surface, prior to covering it with a layer of soil. The fibrous material aids moisture retention to give the germinating seeds a good start, and subsequently rots away. This method of lawn making overcomes the difficulties often encountered when sowing exposed positions and sloping areas but usually precludes the selection of seeds suitable for particular purposes.

Lawns are also established by the use of various dwarf growing plants, which are not grasses, but provide interesting alternatives. See Grass Substitutes.

COMPARATIVE COSTS Establishing a lawn by sowing a good quality grass-seed mixture is undoubtedly the most economical method under most circumstances.

Turf may cost between three and six times as much as seed per square yard of finished lawn area but has the advantage of producing an 'instant' sward. Transport costs are often additional and can add heavily to the cost of turf if it has to be carted for a long distance.

Areas established with dwarf growing ground cover plants will be costlier, depending on the species of plant chosen. Prices are subject to seasonal and market fluctuation and the supplier's location; this makes it unfortunately impossible to give a reliable guide. Always try to obtain a quotation prior to purchase.

Lawn Sand

There are two types of lawn sand, each fulfilling a different function.

The first kills weeds in turf and at the same time stimulates the sward. It consists of one part of sulphate of iron, three parts of sulphate of ammonia and twenty parts of fine sand to act as carrier. See Weeds and Weedkillers.

The second type of lawn sand is used to kill moss and its formulation includes mercury. It is available under a variety of trade names and described as mercurised lawn or turf sand or as mercurised moss killer. See Moss.

Lawn Spreader

A useful tool that facilitates the even distribution of grass seed, fertiliser, weedkiller and top-dressing on turf. Models range from 12in to 24in in width and are constructed in either metal or polypropylene; they are usually fitted with easily interchangeable rollers driven by the landwheels of the spreader. The size and shape of the indentation on the roller surface control application rates of whichever material you happen to be applying to your lawn. A whole series of rollers are available, capable of applying ranges from less than one ounce per square yard to a few pounds, for top-dressing applications (Fig 24).

Use spreaders carefully and systematically in order not to overlap application nor miss any places. Most models are fitted with markers

Fig 24 Lawn spreader

to indicate the areas of lawn already covered; the wheel-tracks of the distributor can also prove a good guide. If possible use a spreader fitted with an on-off control to prevent spillage and excessive applications when starting and turning. To ensure absolute even distribution you may split seeds or dressings into two separate halves by weight, but distribute the second half at right angles to the first Corners of irregularly shaped lawns should be marked off as well as those margins so close to a wall or flower-bed as to make it impossible to start pushing the spreader from the edge of the turf. The main portion of the turf should be treated first and the operation completed by treating the marked-off strips (Fig 25).

Lead Arsenate
A poisonous earthworm expellent, also used for killing other insects infesting lawns and usually applied in solution at a rate of $\frac{1}{2}$-1oz per gal of water, which is sufficient to treat one square yard. Great care must be taken when using this material and children and pets must be kept away from treated areas for a minimum of six weeks after application. Lead arsenate has residual action of four years or longer. It is better to use one of the numerous alternative and safer earthworm expellents and killers on the market. See Earthworms.

63

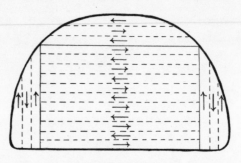

Fig 25 Correct method of using a lawn spreader

Leaf Sweeper

A valuable asset for lawns of reasonable size irrespective of the presence of trees. A leaf sweeper consists of a stiff cylindrical nylon brush from 24-42in long, driven horizontally across the turf by two landwheels. As the machine is pushed forward, the brush revolves and sweeps not only leaves but also small sticks, worm-casts, ant-hills and any other small debris into a canvas or polythene collecting bag. It is much quicker and perhaps more efficient than raking.

Leaf sweepers also collect grass clippings left by rotary mowers without a grass box. A very vital function as mowings left to rot on the turf make it wet and slippery. They also increase the risk of disease and encourage earthworm activity.

Leatherjackets

The very aptly named grubs or larvae of the crane-fly, better known as daddy-longlegs of which there are several species. The 1-1½in larvae vary from greyish-brown to grey-black in colour, are without legs and have an extremely tough, wrinkled skin. They feed almost exclusively on the roots of growing crops including those of grass which results in poor growth, withered patches of turf and the eventual death of the plant. Turf damage is usually most apparent during spring particularly in seasons following a wet autumn.

Crane-flies flying over turf during late summer and early autumn are probably laying eggs, and are often a sign of trouble to come. Starlings working over mature turf should be welcomed as they are usually after the leatherjackets.

The least expensive method of control is to wet affected areas of the lawn thoroughly with water during the evening and then to cover them immediately with black polythene or sacks. The lack of air in the soil makes the larvae rise to the surface during the night and they can then be swept up in the morning or left for the birds to eat. This method is, however, only practical for the smaller areas and may have to be repeated before providing complete control.

BHC (qv) applied in the autumn provides satisfactory control and may be applied at the rate recommended by the manufacturers, either as a dust which has to be well watered in or in liquid form. Chlordane (qv) which is a wormkiller may also be used.

Leaves
Autumn leaves on turf should be raked or swept up regularly. They encourage earthworm activity and the larger leaves, if left to rot on the grass, discolour the turf and increase the likelihood of disease. Use a wire-sprung rake or a besom. Raking and sweeping serve not only to keep the lawn tidy but scarify the turf at the same time. See Leaf Sweeper.

Leontodon species   See Hawkbit

Levelling
This usually involves the movement of a considerable weight of soil and is therefore best carried out during the spring or summer months when the ground is drier and lighter and when the structure of the soil, which under wet conditions is spoilt through excessive consolidation, is better preserved.

It is not necessary initially to pay too much attention to the overall level of the future lawn; only the extreme hollows and mounds need to be dealt with; this will be sufficient to show the surface in its correct perspective, giving an opportunity to visualise whether the lawn shall be flat, sloping or undulating.

Slopes of up to 1 in 50 can be quite attractive without being too difficult to mow and also facilitate natural drainage; steeper slopes lend themselves better to terracing.

Terracing usually calls for extensive deep digging, in which case the top soil must be first removed and stored at some convenient spot for eventual replacement. It should be stacked in shallow heaps to avoid compaction and deterioration of the soil structure.

If it is intended that the lawn should conform to the natural contours of the land, no further levelling is necessary apart from trueing the surface, but where extensive levelling is contemplated, it is not safe to rely on the judgment of the eye if a truly flat surface is to result; instead use level pegs and a spirit level. Level pegs are best made of inch square timber and pointed at one end so that they may be easily driven into the ground. Their length will depend on the gradient of the site, the long ones being driven into the lowest points, the shorter ones into the highest; in most instances 18in long pegs should be adequate. A clearly defined gauge mark should be made 6in from the top of each peg.

To start levelling, select the highest point of the area and drive a short peg into the ground so that the gauge mark is level with the soil. Now drive a second peg in some five or six feet away from the first, but not up to its gauge mark. Next take a plank, long enough to span the two pegs and stand it on edge on top of the two pegs; then place a spirit level on top of the plank. This should reveal that the second peg is higher than the first. If it does, tap the second peg deeper into the ground with a mallet and test again. When the bubble of the spirit level is central, the tops of the two pegs are level (Fig 26).

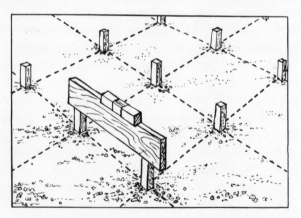

Fig 26 Levelling the ground with pegs, straight edge and spirit level

Repeat this performance all over the area to be levelled, and three or four feet beyond. The result will be a small forest of stakes of which the tops – and therefore their gauge marks – are all level. The depth of filling necessary to bring the overall surface up to the level of the first peg can now be clearly seen. Remember that the perimeter level pegs should be at least three or four feet outside the intended limits, as this will prevent the lawn from sloping untidily at its edges.

Final soil levelling can now be commenced. Start by filling up the lowest lying areas first, gradually working towards an ever more even surface. The soil must be well consolidated and at least a week or ten days be allowed to elapse for natural settlement to take place prior to planting. Failure to consolidate may cause subsidence long after the lawn has been completed and is growing.

Lichen

A flowerless dual organism, part algae and part fungus, usually in the form of dense small leaves. Several different sorts invade turf, some with cinnamon coloured leaves, others varying from greyish-white to nearly black. Wet lichen is apt to make the surface very slippery, but it curls up into small rosette-like shapes when dry. Usually present on turf of poor fertility and with inadequate drainage and aeration; also appears on compacted soils particularly if these are subject to shade and drip from overhanging trees.

Short term control is achieved by applying $\frac{1}{2}$oz of sulphate of iron mixed with 4oz of sand per sq yd. To stop the lichen from re-invading the turf, more permanent measures are necessary, eg feeding the turf, aeration followed by a top dressing of lawn sand and removal of overhanging boughs from trees. See Algae.

Ligule

A usually membraneous out-growth at the bottom of the leaf-blade where it joins the sheath (qv). The ligule is an important aid for the identification of grasses and is clearly illustrated for each of the important turf species mentioned in this volume (Fig 27).

Lime

Fine turf thrives best in slightly acid soils. Lime corrects soil acidity, or sourness as it is sometimes called. Lime also encourages earthworm activity and may lead to weed invasion and a change in the composition of turf grasses.

It is therefore important that soils intended for lawns are not limed unless a soil test (qv) is first carried out.

Excessively acid conditions rarely pertain, but if liming is found to be necessary, use either ground limestone or ground chalk which are the best forms for turf. Apply during autumn and winter at rates from between 2-4oz per sq yd. See pH.

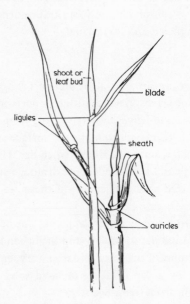

Fig 27 Detail of grass plant

Loam See Soil Preparation

Lolium perenne See Perennial Rye-grass

Lotus corniculatus See Bird's-foot Trefoil

Luzula campestris See Field Wood-rush

Magnesium Sulphate See Epsom Salts

Malachite Green
A green dye capable of controlling fusarium patch (qv) if applied to turf in combination with bordeaux mixture (qv). Rather outdated and superseded by more conveniently handled modern fungicides.

Maleic Hydrazide
A growth regulator (qv) capable of suppressing the growth of grass; not to be used on fine turf.

Manhole Cover
Nothing seems uglier than the very often unavoidable manhole in lawn or terrace. It can soon be turned into a decorative feature by building a three-course-high brick or stone surround; fill this with a mixture of good garden soil and peat for planting out or sowing with annuals. Some garden centres stock pre-fabricated units complete with drainage holes in a variety of finishes which can be filled with earth and used to hide those unsightly inspection covers.

Marasmius oreades
The fungus chiefly responsible for the formation of fairy rings (qv).

Matted Turf
Turf is said to have formed a mat when a layer of vegetative material consisting of living grass leaves and stolons as well as small pieces of lawn clippings and dead fragments of tree leaves have combined into a solid mass and produced an impervious turf surface. If there is doubt as to whether an area of turf is suffering from this problem, the sward should be closely observed after a heavy shower of rain, or 2gal of water sprayed on to 1sq yd of turf through a fine rose. If the water does not readily drain away, mat is the cause. Neglect of this condition leads to weakening of the turf and loss of colour as plants are neither able to obtain moisture nor nutrient.

Check for pH (qv) value and aerate (qv).

MCPA
Known technically as a translocated herbicide, this is a selective

weedkiller suitable for use on turf. Usually available in liquid form under a variety of brand names, it controls many annual and perennial weeds and is particularly effective for eradicating creeping buttercup and plantains.

See Weeds and Weedkillers and also Appendix 3.

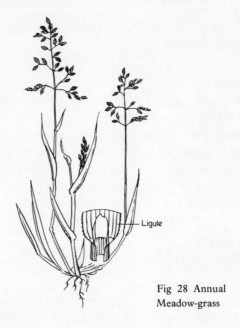

Fig 28 Annual
Meadow-grass

Meadow-grasses

An important group of grasses for special situations belonging to the genus *Poa*.

ANNUAL MEADOW-GRASS *(Poa annua)* An annual or short lived perennial known as annual blue-grass in the USA. It is the most common and widely distributed grass due to its habit of seeding and propagating itself throughout the year. Very dwarf growing, it is present in most lawns and considered a weed in fine turf. Even close mowing is unable to eradicate it because of its habit of forming numerous almost-horizontal flowering and seeding stems which even the mowing machine cutting blade cannot reach (Fig 28).

Annual meadow-grass is, however, useful in situations where it is normally difficult to establish turf and does quite well under trees

Ligule

Fig 29 Rough-stalked Meadow-grass

and in shaded positions even where the soil is compacted. Artificial watering and liming encourages its spread.

No bred cultivars are at the moment on the market and indigenous seed is the best to use. This, unfortunately, has to be obtained from the cleanings from other grass seeds and could possibly include weeds and other impurities. See Purity.

ROUGH-STALKED MEADOW-GRASS *(P. trivialis)* A tufted perennial with leafy stolons useful for moist and shaded areas where heavy soils predominate. Keeps its colour well except if exposed to dry conditions when the foliage turns to reddish-brown. Unable to withstand hard wear (Fig 29).

As there seem to be no well known cultivars available, seedsmen often recommend smooth-stalked meadow-grass or Timothy-grass as an alternative.

SMOOTH-STALKED MEADOW-GRASS *(P. pratensis)* A rhizomatous, erect type of perennial only valuable for second quality lawns. Often used on its own but also in mixtures for sowing road-side verges, banks and playing fields. Its resistance to drought makes it suitable for use on light to medium textured soils. Hard wearing but does not tolerate

71

acid soils nor close mowing. Widely used in the USA where it is known as 'Kentucky blue-grass' (Fig 30).

Some of the usually available cultivars are; 'Baron' – a dwarf growing cultivar bred in Holland, withstands close mowing and keeps its colour well; germinates fairly rapidly after sowing and is resistant to helminthosporium (qv); 'Fylking' – bred in Sweden, rapid establishment, low cutting height tolerance, wears well, resistant to leaf spot diseases; 'Geronimo'–broadish leaves, retains its dark green colour throughout the winter, resistant to rust (qv); 'Modena' – fine leaf, high tillering capacity, can be closely mown; 'Monopoly' – germinates rapidly after sowing and stands up to hard wear, resistant to leaf spot diseases and highly resistant to frost damage; 'Prato' – the cultivar of smooth-stalked meadow-grass which perhaps stands up best to hard wear and close mowing; very persistent, medium to dark green with good resistance to diseases; 'Warrens' – A34 'Kentucky blue-grass' – said to tolerate up to 65 per cent shade when mown at 2in cutting height but can be mown as close as $\frac{3}{8}$in on an open site, originated in USA.

WOOD MEADOW-GRASS *(P. nemoralis)* A perennial, without rhizomes, loosely tufted and indigenous to Europe. Can grow well in shady and damp situations including under trees. Unsuitable for closely-knit, finely-cut turf. Produces charming and delicate seed heads (Fig 31).

'Novombra' is a light green, leafy cultivar which is more compact than many commercial strains.

Mecoprop

A selective herbicide, also known as CMPP, for the control of annual and perennial weeds on established turf. It controls a wide variety of species, including yarrow, clover, pearlwort, creeping buttercup and dandelion in addition to other weeds. It is also offered in combination with 2,4-D. See Weeds and Weedkillers and also Appendix 3.

Medicago lupulina See Black Medick

Mentha pulegium See Pennyroyal and Grass Substitutes

Mercurised Lawn Sand See Lawn Sand

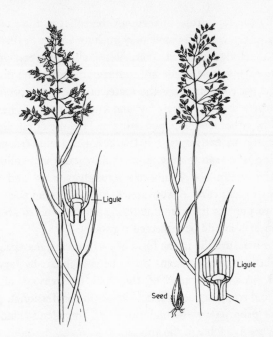

Fig 30 (left) Smooth-stalked Meadow-grass; Fig 31 (right)
Wood Meadow-grass

Mercurous Chloride
A poison, also known as calomel, used for the control of moss (qv) and fungal diseases of turf.

Metaldehyde
A chemical which is used to manufacture slug-killers; usually available in pelleted form.

Methiocarb
A chemical on which certain slug-killers are based.

Moles
The sudden appearance of large earth heaps on the lawn announces the arrival of these animals who spend virtually all their life underground and are little affected by climate. But the mound of earth is not necessarily the first sign indicating their presence;

73

occasionally the turf drops in through the collapse of a burrow just beneath ground level or the mole may push up a ridge of turf.

Moles tunnel vigorously for their diet of slugs, grubs, wireworms, insects and earthworms. They are solitary animals, mate during late winter, and their young leave the maternal home in search of their own territories during late spring and early summer. They can be controlled by either trapping, poisoning and the use of repellents.

Mid-autumn to early spring is the best period for trapping with either a ring-type trap for the more shallow runs and calliper traps for the deeper tunnels. Traps are strongly sprung and must be handled with great care. Always mark and cover trap sites with soil and grass to prevent light from entering tunnels and so alerting the moles; trap sites should be inspected regularly.

Poisoned bait, usually in the form of earthworms, may be placed in runs. Effective poisons can only be obtained by specifically authorised persons, because of this and for reasons of danger, poisoning and trapping moles is best left to the professional.

Various proprietary formulations of repellents and smoke generators are available to the amateur.

Rags soaked in paraffin, creosote or an animal repellent and pushed into the tunnel often provide an effective, although at times only short term, control.

Smoke generators of which there are several types, are usually placed in the runs, lit with a match, and release sulphur and other types of acrid fumes disliked by moles. Other smoke generators produce toxic gasses that actually poison moles in their burrows; use this type of smoke generator with great care and always observe manufacturer's instructions meticulously.

Molluscicide
A chemical preparation to kill or control slugs and snails. See Metaldehyde and Methiocarb.

Morfamquat
A selective weedkiller for use principally on early sown or freshly turfed lawns as well as on mature turf. On newly seeded lawns it controls most common broadleaved weeds. As with other herbicides it

should not be used under drought conditions. See Weeds and Weedkillers and Appendix 3.

Moss

There are hundreds of species of moss and although only a relatively small number of them invade lawns, they all have two means of reproduction and are therefore capable of spreading very rapidly. Sexual reproduction is by means of spores which are particularly abundant during autumn and again in the spring. But mosses also reproduce vegetatively, and any severed part of their stem, leaf or root is capable of developing into another new plant.

It is therefore obvious that one of the greatest fallacies is the often given recommendation that moss should be removed by raking. This is in fact the surest way of spreading it! Similarly never roll mossy turf as this only spreads the spores and fragments of moss to develop into more new plants. The only time to rake moss is when it is dead; that is a few weeks after application of one or other of the various moss killers readily available.

It is often said that mosses only grow in damp situations, many do but there are exceptions, notably the *Polytrichum* species that prefer dry, light and well aerated soils which are deficient in plant foods. Some other mosses show distinct preference for either alkaline or acid soils.

Moss only colonises lawns if growing conditions for the grasses are less than optimum. Its presence is always symptomatic of one or more basic constructional or cultural faults, and until these are corrected, moss cannot permanently be eradicated.

Moss is a flowerless plant and invades heavy and badly drained areas; it spreads on those parts of the lawn which are shaded by either buildings or overhanging trees; it thrives on soils where the surface is too compacted or where the soil lacks nutrients and the grass is starved. Moss also invades grass which is mown too closely.

It is not difficult to kill and eradicate on a permanent basis but correction of any basic fault is the first pre-requisite. Once this has been done, a healthy sward of actively growing grass will usually resist moss invasion. See Soil Preparation, Drainage, Aeration, Fertiliser and Mowing.

Of the several treatments available for the eradication of moss, mercurous chloride is perhaps the most economical and effective, although it is a poison. Obtainable under the name of calomel it can be applied to lawns alone but is best added with lawn sand; the iron sulphate component of the latter aids calomel to provide a more rapid control. Mercurous chloride inhibits spore germination and iron sulphate kills the moss. The complete mixture is often sold as mercurised lawn sand.

There are several proprietary moss killers on the market based on these and other chemicals including chloroxuron and dichlorophen; some even contain fungicides for the control of turf diseases. Still other moss killers are formulated with fertilisers to encourage grasses to take over areas vacated by the dying moss. If this type of preparation is applied during the autumn, select one with little or no nitrogen, as an excess of this fertiliser applied late during the growing season increases the risks of fusarium patch disease (qv).

Moss is usually not much of a problem during the summer months, but spreads more rapidly during autumn and in open winters because it grows better than grass in the less intense light prevailing at that time of the year.

Autumn is consequently the correct time to apply chemical controls which can, if necessary, be followed during the spring with a second application. Unless rain intervenes most moss killers need to be watered in within three days of application.

Some moss killers are water soluble and are best applied through the fine rose or sprinkle-bar of a watering can. Those in dry form can be spread by hand or with a lawn-spreader. If a dry formulation is used, one which is light in colour is much easier to see thus ensuring even spreading. The physical task of applying moss killers is basically no different from spreading or watering weedkiller or fertiliser on to the turf.

Mowers
Of the five basic types of mower, three are of the cylinder or reel type, operating with cutting blades arranged around a horizontally revolving cylinder which moves against a stationary bottom blade and so cuts the grass with scissor-like action. The remainder have a

rotary cutting action, that is with the cutting blades rotating horizontally. Choice of mower must be influenced by the size of the lawn, the required quality of turf and the cost of the machine.

CYLINDER MOWERS The most important point with this type of mower is the number of cutting blades on the cylinders; the more blades, the higher the number of cuts, the better the appearance and quality of the sward.

The side wheel, light-weight, hand-pushed models are the least expensive and most suitable for the small lawn. The cutting cylinder is normally 12-14in wide and fitted with four to six cutting blades. Machines of this type are without rear rollers and ideal for cutting long and rough grass; they also cause the least damage when mowing newly seeded lawns for the first time. The roller mower, still hand propelled, is one step up giving a better finish to the turf and is able to cut right up to the edges of the lawn. Like all machines fitted with a back roller it creates the light and dark green stripe effect so popular with some turf enthusiasts. Individual makers' models have varying degrees of sophistication; driving gears for the cutting cylinders are usually enclosed and ribbed or flat; rollers either in one piece or split to facilitate turning on corners. Cutting widths range from 12-18in with six to twelve knives mounted on the cylinder. The motor mower, apart from the power unit, is basically no different from the hand-propelled roller mower except that it becomes a necessity if large areas have to be mown.

Cutting widths vary from 12-20in and the cutting cylinder usually carries six knives. Roller and knives are driven independently (so that the roller only can be used for moving the machine itself) and are geared to give around 80 cuts per yard, with a speed which can be controlled ranging from one to four miles per hour. A higher number of cuts per yard consumes more power but produces a finer finish; the best and usually most expensive models provide up to 130 cuts per yard whilst a hand-operated machine averages only 30 cuts per yard.

Models may be powered with either 2-stroke or the more easily started 4-stroke petrol engines; some use petrol only and others a petrol/oil mixture. Electrically operated mowers are equally efficient; those powered by mains electricity suffer from the disadvantage of trailing cables although spring operated cable-winding drums which automatically take up any slack cable are now fitted to some machines. Be careful not to allow the cable anywhere near the cutting blades! Battery-operated mowers are becoming increasingly popular and are ideal and convenient machines to use. They have low running and maintenance costs and always start instantly at the flick of a switch. Like petrol-driven models they provide the turf with a good finish, are just as quick in operation as mains-electric powered mowers but naturally need a new battery every two or three years. The battery needs to be recharged after each mowing and, if in good condition, is capable of storing sufficient energy for about two hours continuous mowing.

ROTARY MOWERS These are always powered with either a petrol engine or by mains electricity. They are fitted with horizontally rotating knives that cut the grass with an action similar to a scythe. The design and capabilities of rotary mowers have improved a great deal since they were first introduced and the latest models are quite suitable for cutting the average lawn. Many types are available with cutting widths ranging from 12-20in. Some machines are fully power-driven whilst on others the motor drives only the cutting blades and the mower has to be hand propelled across the grass. This is not necessarily a bad thing for the slower the machine moves, the better the cut.

For really fine turf use one of the very latest rotaries with front and rear rollers, rear-mounted grass collecting box and rapid height of cut adjustment. These are capable of providing nearly as good a finish as a cylinder mower. Rotary mowers have other advantages too. Unlike cylinder mowers they can operate when the lawn is a little damp and the grass a little longer than it should be. The same machines can also cope with very much rougher and longer grass in paddocks and orchards or tackle the mass of vegetation left when naturalised bulbs are dying down.

No tough-stalked weeds or grasses escape the rotary blades but unfortunately they do blunt rather rapidly and need re-sharpening every four weeks during the cutting season.

Rotary mowers riding over the turf on a cushion of air operate exactly like the conventional rotaries but as they have no frictional resistance are much lighter to handle. This makes them ideal tools for cutting grass on banks and slopes. They can cut grass up to 12in high even if tangled, matted and wet. The only disadvantage is the lack of a grass box which means that mowings have to be raked up after cutting.

MAINTENANCE OF MOWERS Operate and look after them according to makers' instructions. Immediately after use, wipe the mower down with a rag slightly impregnated with oil. Pay particular attention to the cutting blades and keep them clean and shiny at all times. Free the machine of all loose grass and scrape soil and grass from rollers. Always store the machine in a dry place and under cover. Send the mower away periodically for service and overhaul and have the blades re-set and sharpened annually during the winter season.

Mowing

Mowing has to be repeated between thirty and fifty times per year and the period between cuts and the height of the grass influence the quality of the sward.

HEIGHT OF CUT The natural tendency of any plant, including grass, is to reproduce itself by throwing up seedheads. Regular mowing prevents this and encourages grasses to throw out further blades from their roots instead, thereby thickening the sward and ensuring their own continuance.

Cutting the turf too closely brings about the opposite results. The mower blades bite deep into the grass and in severe cases can cause irreparable damage by cutting the root crowns. The leaves are almost wholly shaved off and can no longer fulfil the necessary function of collecting the vital elements from the air so essential for efficient growth. The resultant turf is loosely knit and open to weed and moss invasion; its colour and resistance to drought is poor and bald patches quickly develop if it is subjected to any kind of wear.

The height of cut for lawns consisting of the finer growing grasses is best aimed at $\frac{3}{8}-\frac{1}{2}$in and from $\frac{3}{4}$-1in for the utility lawn.

SETTING THE MOWER The mower is easily set for any height of cut. First turn the machine upside down with the bottom fixed blade (sole plate) uppermost. In the case of side wheel machines, place a straight edge from the back roller to the lowest points of each side wheel. The

79

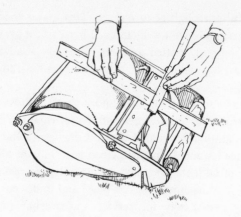

Fig 32 Setting a mower for height of cut

distance between the straight edge and the cutting side of the sole plate determines the height of cut and is easily altered by lowering or heightening the back roller position (Fig 32).

A roller mower is similarly adjusted but the straight edge is placed from the front to the rear roller. The distance between the straight edge and sole plate must be the same on each side of the lawn mower, or it will cut unevenly.

SCARIFYING PRIOR TO MOWING However well set and sharp the mower is, it will not cut every blade at the pre-set height. Many are pushed or trodden into the ground, creeping weeds intertwine in the grass and dead vegetation accumulates. At monthly intervals, just prior to mowing, light scarification with a wire rake aerates the turf, sets up grass and weeds for the mower and generally invigorates the lawn. Raking also scatters worm casts which must otherwise be brushed before every cut, or the mower presses them into unsightly circles of compact soil through which the finer grasses cannot penetrate.

If the grass is wet but must be mown, first brush it with a besom. Avoid mowing if the ground is soft from rain, particularly if a side-wheel machine is used. These are apt to leave the turf ridged with wheel marks.

FREQUENCY OF MOWING Commence mowing during the early spring, when the grass shows the first sign of growth, and let subsequent cuts be timed by the speed of grass growth. If a fine sward is desired, this alone must be the deciding factor. Mowing the lawn at a certain predetermined day of each week, is a mistake many gardeners make, quite ignoring the fact that grass growth depends on moisture supply and the prevailing temperature. Two or even three cuts per week may be necessary during warm and humid conditions, but during early spring or autumn one cut per week may well be sufficient and cold winds during those periods of the year can prolong the interval to 10 to 12 days. Never allow the grass to grow longer than $\frac{1}{4}$in above the ideal height, and preferably only $\frac{1}{8}$in.

The worst punishment a lawn can receive is to cut it too short at long prolonged intervals. Intermittent cutting removes a greater weight of leaves over the whole of a growing season, than more frequent cuts correctly timed, with a consequent greater, although unnecessary, loss of plant food from the soil. The comparatively larger proportion of leaves removed at each infrequent cut also inhibits the plants and leads to sparse and coarse turf of poor colour.

Never allow the lawn to look untidy and ragged and continue cutting during autumn, and even during dry and mild periods in the winter, particularly if the turf contains coarse grasses. They are at their weakest then, and, as they reach their dormant stage long before their finer leaved neighbours, are effectively discouraged during that time.

Mow less frequently than normal during periods of drought, when growth rate is naturally slowed, and increase the normal height of cut from $\frac{1}{8}$–$\frac{1}{4}$in. The denser and longer cover conserves soil moisture and protects the grass roots from the hot sun.

MOW IN ALL DIRECTIONS Every mowing should be carried out in a different direction, to permit the machine to pick up and cut the grass from all angles. After mowing from north to south, change to north-east and south-west and so on around all positions of the compass as far as the shape and situation of the lawn permits.

Mow the sides of the lawn first to allow room to turn the mower when cutting in a regular pattern across the area. The machine must be adjusted to move easily across the turf with only reasonable pushing power. Never use downward pressure on the mower handles and do not proceed by short alternate backwards and forward movements or the sward suffers. If the machine is not capable of working any other way, the blades probably need sharpening or even a complete overhaul is due.

The regular pattern of alternate dark and light green stripes often seen on lawns is not produced by side wheel machines but only by the large roller fitted on the heavier types of mowers. The roller presses the grasses in the direction of its forward movement so that alternate cutting widths have grasses facing in opposite directions; they in turn reflect the light differently and so give the illusion of a striped lawn.

GRASS CUTTINGS Always fit the mower with a box to collect the grass cuttings. Great controversy centres on this point and a number of gardeners advocate that the cuttings, if left on the lawn, rot down and add humus to the ground, which in turn benefits subsequent grass growth.

Theoretically, the argument is correct. In practice, lawn mowings are best removed as the growing grass below them tends to become yellow and earth-worm activity is encouraged. Mowings also tend to stick to shoes and are then carried all over the garden and into the house. It is much better to carry grass cuttings off the lawn, compost them and then return them in the form of a top dressing in due course of time.

Make an exception during periods of drought when the cuttings left on the lawn shield the growing grass from the sun.

AFTER MOWING Clean the mower immediately after use and wipe the cutting blades with an oil impregnated cloth. Be careful to scrape caked soil and clippings from the rollers as an accumulation of these spoil the surface of the lawn and prevent the machine from cutting at its pre-set height.

Never oil or re-fuel a mower when it is standing on the lawn, as both spilt oil and petrol scorch the grass.

Mowrah meal

An efficient and non-poisonous (except to fish) earthworm expellent applied to turf during preferably damp weather in autumn or spring. Use the more efficient, finely ground grades and apply evenly at a rate of 4-8oz per sq yd and water copiously immediately afterwards, preferably with the pressure of a hose so that the the meal is washed thoroughly into the ground.

Mowrah meal, provided it is finely ground, can also be mixed with water and sprayed on to the grass. The suspension soon settles and must be kept well agitated during application.

Worms rise to the surface soon after application and should be swept up.

See Earthworms.

Mushrooms See Fungi

Mycelium
The non-fruiting, vegetative part of a fungus.

Naturalising
This is the cultivation of plants in an artificially created environment closely approximating their natural habitat. It is often practised on lawns under-planted, for example, with daffodils which are left undisturbed between flowering periods each spring. This, however, presents a problem with mowing as daffodils only continue flowering every year if their foliage is left to die naturally, and the area must be left unmown for several weeks.

It is therefore necessary to choose very carefully where the bulbs are to be planted. They will cause the minimum of trouble, and also look their best if planted under trees overhanging turf, although a shaded corner near a shrubbery or hedge, or an orchard may also prove convenient. Do not plant them in first class turf because daffodil leaves are unlikely to wither before early summer when the grass could already be 6in or more in height. The more shaded the area, the longer it takes for daffodil leaves to wither completely; if they are cut too early, the development of the bulb is impaired and fewer flowers result the following year. Similarly never spray weedkiller on to turf planted with bulbs unless their leaves are completely wilted. Once the leaves have dried off, and depending on the size of the area, foliage and grass can be cut close to the ground with a rotary mower, scythe or shears. The remaining vegetation is likely to look yellow-brown and recovery can be speeded by applying a light dressing of nitrogenous fertiliser.

Take care when planting bulbs to arrange them in natural drifts. Just scatter the bulbs indiscriminately over the ground and plant each one exactly where it has come to rest.

Bulbs are easily planted with a spade, push the blade into the ground up to a depth of 3-5in (the bigger the bulb the deeper it needs to be planted), lever up the turf by tilting the spade at an angle of about 45°, slip the bulb underneath and replace and firm the turf. Alternatively use a bulb planter, available from most hardware stores, or in light soils, a home made one from an empty soup or coffee tin, with both ends cut out. Place the tin on the turf where the bulb is to be planted, press it with the foot to cut a circle of soil which is easily removed by working the tin backwards and forwards. Lightly fork the soil at the base of the hole, insert the bulb and replace the core of soil, with the circle of grass on top, and firm.

Nettles
The very common dead nettle *(Lamium purpureum)* is no trouble on turf and quickly disappears during mowing. The stinging nettle *(Urtica dioica)* although rarely found on lawns, can be checked with selective weedkillers. See Weeds and Weedkillers and Appendix 3.

Nitrate of Potash   See Potassium Nitrate

Nitrogen (N)
Nitrogen promotes growth and good colour in turf and is therefore an important element in the feeding programme. It is best used in combination with phosphate and potash but can be applied alone as a booster to turf at the rate of $\frac{1}{2}$oz per sq yd in the form of sulphate of ammonia (qv).

'A little and often' should be the rule with nitrogen applications; too much nitrogen causes lush and soft growth and makes grasses more susceptible to diseases and less able to satisfactorily withstand the autumn and winter months. Nitrogen should never be applied after mid-summer.

Slow-release nitrogen fertilisers are now available and only one application suffices for the season. Applied during early spring, the fertiliser provides an initial boost of nitrogen to the sward and continues to supply this vital nutrient slowly and continuously over a period of three to six months.

See Fertilisers and Feeding and Soil Testing.

Node
The part of a stem from which one or more leaves arise.

Offset
A term often used for a young plant which is vegetatively produced and then split from its parent plant.

Ophiobolus Patch
Ophiobolus graminis. A fungal disease of turf also known as take all. First appears usually during the late summer, autumn and winter in the form of light-brown, small, circular depressions only a few inches in diameter. These are apt to expand and coalesce to form large irregularly shaped areas with the sparsely populated depression being invaded by weeds and weed grasses.

Wet, alkaline soils encourage this disease which usually attacks bents but leaves fescues unaffected.

Ophiobolus patch can only be positively identified by microscopic examination and is often confused with fusarium patch (qv). When attacks are spotted early, dig out the offending patches, fill with fresh soil and either turf or re-seed.

Application, as per makers' recommendations, of phenylmercuric acetate (qv) applied at fortnightly intervals may offer some control. Spring dressings of sulphate of ammonia, which encourage the acidity of the soil, are also of benefit.

Orchard Grass See Cocksfoot

Paraquat
A contact and translocated herbicide which is poisonous, but controls a wide range of annual weeds and grasses, also checks perennials by scorching their tops. See Soil Preparation.

Parsley Piert
Aphanes arvensis. An annual weed which prefers light, dry soils.

Small, pale green with a deeply lobed leaf. A combination of mecoprop and ioxynil can keep it in check. See, Weeds and Weedkillers and Appendix 3.

Patching

If a patch of grass has been damaged, perhaps by the accidental spilling of petrol, or a patch of coarse grass is disfiguring the sward, cut the offending piece of turf out and remove it. Spike the bare ground, remove any weed-roots and refill with new soil and re-seed. Make certain that a grass seed mixture that matches the existing turf is used.

It is often a wise plan to establish a small turf nursery in an otherwise vacant corner of the garden. Sow it with the same grass seed mixture that was used to establish your lawn and so provide instant patches for any repair work.

PCNB

The fungicide quintozene (qv) for the control of turf diseases, is occasionally referred to by these initials; they are an abbreviation of its full chemical name, Pentachloronitrobenzene.

Pearlwort

Sagina procumbens. A weed, if present in fine turf, but which is also capable of making a rich green and dense sward if planted on its own. See Grass Substitute.

It can spread quite rapidly in fine textured turf and in such situations is best controlled with application of selective weedkillers. Mecoprop applied on its own, or mixed with 2,4-D affords control. See Weeds and Weedkillers and Appendix 3.

Lawn sand, too, provides a good control but acts more efficiently if preceded with an application of general fertiliser given as soon as spring growth commences.

Peat

Peat consists of partially decomposed plant remains and when applied to soils improves their texture, be they light, medium or heavy. Application of 6-8lb per sq yd of peat forked into the top 9in of soil rapidly corrects the excess alkalinity of chalky soils and improves and opens up cold, wet and sticky clay soils.

Sedge Peat (1-2lb per sq yd well brushed in) also provides a useful top dressing (qv) for turf either on its own or mixed with fertiliser; it is equally useful for brushing into the crevices between newly laid turves.

Peat Soils See Soil Preparation

Pennyroyal
Mentha pulegium. A weed if present in fine turf, but one which is

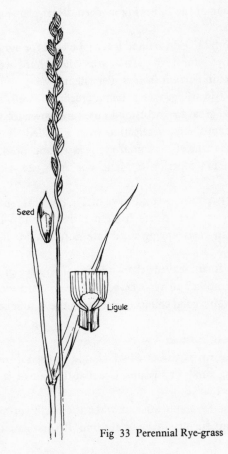

Seed

Ligule

Fig 33 Perennial Rye-grass

87

also capable of producing a thick, deep green, peppermint-scented sward if planted on its own. See Grass Substitutes.

Perennial Rye-grass

Lolium perenne. A tufted, non-creeping perennial with a shiny under-surface to the leaves. Stands up well to hard wear but does not like very close mowing. Used in many grass seed mixtures for sportsfields and hard service lawns. Grows well on most types of free-draining and fertile soils except the very lightest; does not like competition from the bent grasses, nor acid conditions (Fig 33).

The choice of the correct cultivar is all important with rye-grass. There are now many old and out-dated strains which should be ignored in favour of the following modern dwarf-growing and much leafier cultivars.

'Aberystwyth S23' – dwarf and leafy type bred for agricultural use but now employed for turf particularly where hard wear and low maintenance are important factors. Persistent.

'Barenza' – dwarf growing habit, recovers well after heavy treading. A good grass for inclusion in mixtures sown for winter use.

'Kent Indigenous' and a selection from it called 'Romney' have smaller seeds than most perennial rye-grasses and produce a dense sward. They are not superior to 'Melle' nor 'Aberystwyth S23' under heavy wear.

'Melle' – perhaps the best cultivar of the prostrate growing leafy perennial rye-grass. Persistent, drought resistant and winter hardy. Grows well from early spring until late autumn. Medium to dark green.

'Stadion' – finer leaved than many other rye-grasses, good persistency and ability to recover quickly from hard wear. Disease resistant and retains good colour even during the winter season.

Permanganate of Potash

The only earthworm expellent which should be used if there is a risk of contaminating ponds or streams. Use it at the rate of $\frac{1}{2}$oz per gal of water applied to 1 sq yd.

Optimum time for application is when the earthworms are active and the soil damp during spring or autumn. Permanganate of potash also referred to as potassium permanganate is less effective than mowrah meal (qv).

Petrol
Never re-fuel, oil or clean lawnmowers on turf. Even slight spillage of petrol and oil are apt to stain and discolour the grass, or worse, cause brown patches.

pH
The acidity or alkalinity of soils is measured on what is known as the pH scale. Soils range from the most acid sands of pH 3.0 to acid peat of pH 4.0 right through the spectrum to the upper limits of chalky soils of pH 8.5. The neutral point is pH 7.0.

pH values are based on a logarithmic scale which means that pH 5.0 is ten times more acid than pH 6.0 and pH 8.5 ten times more alkaline than pH 7.5.

Fine lawn grasses grow best under acid conditions, pH value from 6.0 to 6.5. Higher levels tend to encourage the growth of meadow grasses which are not always desirable constituents of fine turf. Below pH 6.0 application of lime is essential to strong growth. Excess of lime, on the other hand, can be counteracted by repeated applications of sulphate of ammonia or sulphate of iron but these should be spread gradually over a period. This effect can be heightened by using lime-free sand and occasional dressings of peat.

Phenylmercuric Acetate
PMA. Used as a fungicide to control dollar spot, fairy rings, fusarium patch, ophiobolus patch and red thread (qv). Available under a number of brand names, this material must be handled carefully and strictly in accordance with makers' instructions. It is an organic compound of mercury and is poisonous. Always wear gloves when using it and immediately wash off any accidental splashes on the skin (which can cause unpleasant and painful rashes or blisters) with soap and water. Use a safer material whenever possible. Phenylmercurial Acetate damages or kills smooth-stalked meadow-grass (qv) and should therefore not be applied to swards containing this species.

Phleum pratense See Timothy-grass; also known as cat's-tail.

Phosphate (P)
A vital ingredient in a balanced fertiliser which should also include nitrogen and potash. Phosphate encourages root growth, assists respiration and adds to the general well-being of the plant. Super-phosphate is the most suitable type for application to turf, normally at the rate of 1oz per sq yd. See Fertilisers and Feeding also Soil Testing.

Photosynthesis
A process whereby water and carbon dioxide are combined in green plants to form complex carbohydrates and proteins through the energy of sunlight. The chlorophyll (qv) present in the plant performs a vital function in the absorption of sunlight and the utilisation of its energy.

Phyllopertha horticola See Chafer Grub

Plantago species See Plantains

Fig 34 (left) Broad-leaved Plantain; Fig 35 (right) Ribwort Plantain

Plantains

Easily recognised by their spike of minute flowers, they are objectionable weeds on any lawn. Most types are fortunately easily controlled with selective weedkillers.

GREATER PLANTAIN *(Plantago major)* has large oval leaves with prominent parallel veins and rats-tail-like, erect, green flower spikes; often common in poor meadow turf (Fig 34).

HOARY PLANTAIN *(P. media)* is capable of growing to a height of 12 in, has downy leaves and occurs on chalky soils.

RIBWORT PLANTAIN *(P. lanceolata)* has narrower leaves which form rosettes; very common (Fig 35).

SEA PLANTAIN *(P. maritima)* is a more woody plant and prefers sea-side locations like salt marshes. Frequently present in Cumberland and sea-washed turf.

STARWEED OR BUCKS-HORN PLANTAIN *(P. coronopus)* is found near coasts and is distinguished by its flat, starfish-like rosettes of deeply divided, single-veined, narrow leaves. See Weeds and Weedkillers and Appendix 3.

Planting a Lawn

The planting of grass roots is often the only method of producing lawns in less temperate climates and has long been practised with tropical grasses which bear coarse and heavily ribbed blades.

Ground preparations are exactly the same as for other lawn making methods and although planting is a little more laborious than seeding it takes less time and effort than turfing.

WHEN TO PLANT Autumn or spring. If you plant during the autumn little visible growth takes place but the roots, often called stolons (qv) or offsets, are able to establish themselves to get a good start over spring planted lawns. If the season is dry, spring plantings are liable to mature a month later but even then form usable turf by late summer.

GROWING ROOTS Sow stoloniferous bent grasses in a vacant corner in your garden, permit them to grow both sideways and upwards, only keeping the seed heads clipped. If sown during early spring or autumn you will soon have sufficient stolons or offets to plant as described below.

PURCHASE OF ROOTS The live roots have a very limited shelf life and are therefore not stocked in shops. They are only obtainable from specialists who arrange to have supplies of nursery roots sent direct to your home.

DELIVERY OF ROOTS To prevent moisture losses the roots are packed in polythene (or individually rooted in small pots) and look like a big ball of tangled knitting wool. Do not be disappointed by their appearance as at this stage, with their few green and rather coarse leaves, they give no indication or hint of the final lawn.

If you cannot plant the roots immediately, store them in a dark and cool place where they will keep satisfactorily for up to seven days. If planting is likely to be delayed even longer it is advisable to 'heel' them in. Remove the roots from the polythene bag and soak them in cold water from 12 to 24 hours. Then dig a narrow trench on vacant and preferably shaded ground no deeper than 3in and spread the roots along it. Cover lightly with soil so that some of the roots are still showing and water regularly to prevent their drying out. Treated in this manner they will be safe for several weeks.

PLANTING Prior to planting, the roots must be divided into correctly sized portions for each of the planting positions spaced at 12in intervals right across the ground. Gently tease the bundle of roots apart and break off four or five pieces each some four to six inches long. There is no need to mark out the ground, prior to planting, simply dig a trowel into the soil 6in away from the lawn boundary and 1½in deep. Ease the trowel gently forward and backward in the soil to form a narrow trench. Place one of the previously divided portion of roots into the trench and at the back of the trowel, allowing the roots to protrude a little from each end. Now remove the

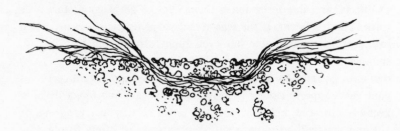

Fig 36 Planting stolons or runners

92

trowel and with your foot press the soil round the small trench firm and level. Make sure the roots are really firmly settled, particularly in light soils, or birds are apt to pull them up for nesting material!

Repeat this process at 12in intervals along the whole length of the first row. Plant the next row 12in from the first but stagger your planting so that no two plants in neighbouring rows are opposite each other (Fig 36).

To obtain compact turf never plant the roots more than 12in apart, but if you wish for more rapid turf formation, decrease the normal planting distances to 9in or even 6in.

A light roller pushed over the ground after planting, provided the soil is not too wet, helps to firm the roots and aids the protuding shoots to root by pressing them firmly to the ground.

WATERING Water immediately after rolling and keep on watering whenever the weather necessitates it. Even then some runners may die, but do not worry as you have planted four to five at every position to allow for just such an eventuality.

WEEDS Weeds and weed grasses must be pulled out. The careful and shallow use of a hoe between the rows of growing grass, not only kills the weeds, but keeps the uppermost soil surface in a fine condition for the spreading runners to root into. Once the runners are beginning to meet in the rows, hoeing must of course cease. Continue to hand weed and do not use weedkillers during the first six to eight weeks, and after that only in strict accordance with manufacturers' instructions.

TURF FORMATION The early growth is straggly with runners rooting themselves to the ground from every node and at the same time spreading across the ground in all directions. Leaf growth is coarse and sparse, and while some runners remain in lateral positions, others suddenly commence to grow at an angle of 30°. This is the signal for mowing to commence as cutting at this stage increases the number of spreading shoots. With the mower's sharp cutting blades set high, just top the growth and repeat twice weekly if necessary. Make sure you do not cut the stolons creeping over the surface as they are the foundation of your lawn.

Even before the ground is completely covered and a week or so after the first cut, apply a top dressing. Use a mixture of finely sifted soil and peat and apply evenly over the whole surface at the rate of $1\frac{1}{2}$ to 2lb per sq yd. Never use lawn sand on a lawn made from stoloniferous grasses as it is inclined to burn the runners.

As the growing season progresses the grass blades fine down and become narrower and more closely packed until the lawn gradually assumes its adult characteristics.

MOWING When the turf is mature it must be cut regularly although less frequently than most lawns. As a considerable portion of the root system lies only just below the green leaves, close cuts must never be taken. If you cut low enough to damage the runners the lawn will die off. Start mowing with the cutting blades $1\frac{1}{2}$in from ground level and gradually reduce during succeeding cuts to arrive at a height of $\frac{1}{2}$in or $\frac{3}{4}$in at the end of the season.

Persistent cutting of the grass at too high a level is equally bad, as it will build up into a thick mat and so lift the fine leaves forming the lawn surface further and further away from their food and moisture supply. The appearance of brown patches soon makes this mistake obvious and this is best corrected by cutting the lawn quite ruthlessly and low enough to expose all the surface runners. A lawn treated in this manner soon recovers its original colour and density particularly if helped by a top dressing.

UPKEEP With exception of the already stated differences, never to use lawn sand and to mow slightly higher than normal, there is little difference between the maintenance and management of this type of lawn as compared with others.

PMA

Phenylmercuric acetate (qv) a poisonous chemical used as a fungicide for the control of turf diseases.

Poa species See Meadow-grass

Polygonum aviculare See Knotgrass

Potash (K)

The potassium content of fertiliser promotes firm, healthy growth and helps plants to withstand diseases. Turf does not require large amounts, and it is usually incorporated with nitrogen and phosphate

in the form of sulphate of potash. Recommended rate $\frac{1}{4}$oz per sq yd.
See Fertiliser and Feeding also Soil Testing.

Potassium Nitrate
An expensive fertiliser also known as saltpetre containing both
nitrogen and potash in readily available form. Ideal for liquid feeding
of lawns at the rate of $\frac{1}{2}$oz per gal of water.

Potassium Permanganate See Permanganate of Potash

Potassium Sulphate See Sulphate of Potash

Potentilla anserina See Silverweed

Potentilla reptans See Cinquefoil

Pre-emergence Damping-off
A term used to describe the lack of emergence of young seedlings
from freshly sown seed. The failure is usually due to fungal infection.
See Seedling Diseases.

Pre-seeding Fertiliser
Dress the soil with a well balanced fertiliser a few days before sowing
and rake it into the top two inches of soil. A good mixture consists of
2 parts by weight of sulphate of ammonia, 4 parts superphosphate
and 1 part of sulphate of potash.

Any of the good proprietary pre-seeding fertilisers on the market
will act equally well, though they may prove a little more expensive.

Prostrate
A plant with non-rooting stem growing horizontally along the
ground is of prostrate habit of growth.

Prunella vulgaris See Self-heal

Puccinia coronata See Rust

Purity
A term used to express, as a percentage, the number of pure named
seeds present in a given sample. Weed seeds and inert matter such as

dirt and chaff are naturally classed as impurities. Never buy seeds of bred cultivars of less than 99 per cent purity.

Pythium See Seedling Diseases (qv)

Quack-grass See Couch

Quintozene
A fungicide for the control of fusarium patch, dollar spot and red thread (qv) in fine turf.

Ranunculus acris See Crowfoot

Ranunculus bulbosus See Buttercup

 Ranunculus ficaria See Celandine, Lesser

Ranunculus repens See Buttercup

Red Creeping Fescue
Festuca rubra subspecies *rubra* also known as creeping fescue or red fescue. See Fescues.

Red Fescue See Fescues

Red Thread
Corticium fuciforme. A fungal disease of turf liable to appear during the growing season but more usually not until late summer. Grass leaves and stems carry patches of pink or red fungus which can, during the late stages, develop into small, spiked, coral-like outgrowths located near the leaf tip. Red thread is unlikely to kill the grass but is unsightly especially during humid weather when the fungus on the grass and ground may be gelatinous.

Red fescue is apt to suffer heavy attacks but brown top, perennial rye-grass and annual meadow-grass although susceptible, suffer less severely.

Cultural controls include adequate aeration and application of nitrogen, which should only be given during the spring and early summer. If the disease is present in only mild form during the early part of the year, a dressing of nitrogen fertiliser may be sufficient to help the grass overcome the infection. Chemical control measures are exactly the same as those for fusarium patch (qv).

Renovation

Provided there is still some grass growing, most neglected areas of turf are capable of renovation, and big improvements can be brought about in little more than one season by systematically carrying out the necessary tasks in correct sequence.

Start renovation work during either autumn or spring by cutting the grass, but not too closely. If operations are started during the autumn there is little that can be done except scarifying and aeration of the ground and application of a good quantity of top-dressing. If operations are begun during spring, follow the same procedure but apply a good dressing of fertiliser after aeration. Mow whenever necessary and apply weedkiller when the temperature begins to rise. Mid-summer is the correct time for another application of fertiliser followed two weeks later with a second weedkiller application to rid the turf of the more persistent weeds. Follow with more aeration during the autumn and a liberal application of top dressing. If the grass is still thin, mix $\frac{1}{2}$-1oz of grass seed per sq yd into the top dressing.

Simultaneously with these operations, carry out any required repair work during the spring and summer months; ridding the lawn of bumps and hollows, patching turf and trimming the edges.

Many new houses built on agricultural land may be sited on old meadows and these too can be made into respectable turf if treated as just described.

See Aeration, Bumps and Hollows, Fertiliser, Patching, Top Dressing, Weeds and Weedkillers.

Rhizome

A more or less horizontal underground stem with scale-like leaves throwing up new stems at intervals, eg couch and creeping fescue (Fig 37).

Rollers and Rolling

Alternating frost and thaw in addition to heavy winter rains, cause

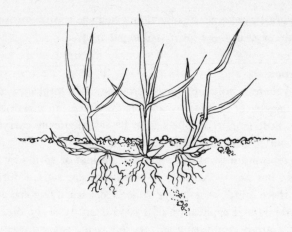

Fig 37 A rhizomatic grass

the movement of soil particles so that by early spring some grass roots may no longer be in firm contact with the soil and therefore unable to take up adequate supplies of moisture and plant foods. This set of circumstances provides the only occasion when a roller should be used on a lawn. During the rest of the year, the use of a roller-mower and general walking on the lawn automatically looks after its needs for consolidation. Sweep the lawn before rolling to scatter wormcasts and to remove stones and other winter debris. Do not use a roller heavier than 1cwt and when rolling, always do so twice, the second time in a direction at right angles to the first. Always draw the roller slowly across the surface, and never roll the lawn when the grass is wet or during periods of drought.

A roller will not level uneven lawns; it only consolidates the soil on the raised parts excessively, handicaps the roots of the grass and, during subsequent dry spells, causes wide and deep cracks in the ground.

Rough-stalked Meadow-grass See Meadow-grass

Royal Horticultural Society
Any person interested in gardening is eligible to apply for Fellowship and thereby derives many benefits for a very reasonable annual fee:

tickets for admission to Chelsea Flower Show and the twenty or so other shows held every year, admission to the Society's garden at Wisley, a copy of the Society's monthly journal and the use of its library and the right to borrow books by post. Fellows may also obtain advise on horticultural problems including the identification of plants and the control of pests and diseases. It is also possible, subject to certain fees and limitations, to obtain analysis of manure, soils etc and to have fruit identified.

Fellowship of the Society is recommended to everyone keenly interested in gardening and they should apply to the Secretary, Royal Horticultural Society, Vincent Square, London SW1P 2PE.

Rumex acetosa See Sorrel

Rumex acetosella See Sorrel

Rumex (other species) See Docks

Runner See Stolon

Rye grass See Perennial Rye-grass and Seed Mixtures

Rust
Puccinia coronata. Recognised by rust spots on both the top and underside of leaves of grasses, usually during autumn, which yellow and die prematurely. Applications of potash and phosphate fertiliser usually remedy the situation.

Sagina procumbens See Pearlwort and Grass Substitutes

Saltpetre
The common name for potassium nitrate (qv) also known as nitrate of potash.

Scarifying See Aeration

Sclerotinia homoeocarpa See Dollar Spot

Scutch See Couch

Sea Milkwort
Glaux maritima. A tiny leaved, prostrate perennial weed with pink

flowers mostly found near coasts. Usually imported inland with sea-washed turf. Selective herbicides provide good control. See Weeds and Weedkillers, also Appendix 3.

Sea Pink

Armeria maritima. A tufted perennial weed also known as thrift and similar in leaf to the sea plantain which likes the same coastal environment. Selective weedkillers control it well. See Weeds and Weedkillers, also Appendix 3.

Seed-borne

Carried on or in seed; usually referring to disease organisms.

Seed Counts

Approximate number of seeds per lb. Allowance must be made for the various cultivars within a species as seed sizes vary, especially so with perennial rye-grass.

	Approximate no. of seeds per lb +/− 15%
Annual meadow-grass	2,000,000
Brown top	4,500,000
Chewings fescue	450,000
Cocksfoot	480,000
Creeping bent	4,800,000
Crested dog's-tail	750,000
Fine-leaved sheep's fescue	550,000
Hard fescue	500,000
Perennial rye-grass	260,000
Red fescue	450,000
Rough-stalked meadow-grass	2,200,000
Sheep's fescue	1,100,000
Smooth-stalked meadow-grass	2,200,000
Timothy-grass	1,100,000
Velvet bent	5,000,000
Wavy hair-grass	800,000
Wood meadow-grass	2,000,000

Seed Dressing

The application of a chemical, in either dust or liquid form to the seed in order to protect it from disease and from damage caused by birds eating the freshly sown seeds.

There are a number of proprietary chemicals available and seedsmen usually sell already treated grass-seed mixtures or will have them dressed if requested.

Captan and thiram (qv) are useful materials for protecting seeds from fungal attack and also keep birds at bay. Ever better materials are continually being formulated and seedsmen's current recommendations are likely to be correct.

Always wash your hands carefully after you have handled chemically treated seed; never allow it to come into contact with children or animals and do not permit sacks or containers which have held treated seed to be used for other purposes. Both captan and thiram can be irritating to skin and harmful to fish. Always apply any chemical strictly according to manufacturer's instructions.

Seed Mixtures

Most existing lawns are deliberate or accidental mixtures of different types of grasses. A single species seldom makes a good lawn and usually increases management difficulties and maintenance costs. It is almost impossible to keep indigenous or volunteer grasses from creeping into any lawn and they will be particularly noticeable and create an ugly focal point in turf made from only one species of grass. An example would be a lawn sown with very fine and slender-leaved Chewings fescue interspersed by indigenous broad-leaved and fairly coarse perennial rye-grass.

In practice, seed mixtures of two or more compatible grasses are usually sown in an endeavour to produce a tightly-knit turf that prevents invasion from weeds and other grasses.

The individual grasses in the mixtures are chosen to complement each other in growth habit, disease susceptibility and general compatibility. Fescues and bents are ideal companions because both stand up well to repeated close cutting and are slower to germinate and grow than the rye and meadow-grasses. Each group also serves a different purpose; fescues and bents are ideal dwarf growing grasses

101

for fine lawns, golf and even bowling greens, whereas rye and meadow-grasses usually have to be cut more frequently, are less permanent and are better suited for hockey pitches, outfields or a piece of ground used as a children's play area.

Beware of seed mixtures consisting of too many species and cultivars which are only included on the principle that some will survive and prove suitable. Any individual grass representing less than 10 per cent of the mixture is unlikely to be very noticeable in the resulting sward. If too many species are sown, some will never come up and the turf is apt to be patchy in colour and texture and the desirable, slower growing, non-agressive species tend to be smothered by the coarser, broad-leaved but more aggressive types. The turf may still appear to be quite normal for a little while after sowing, but within a season or two the balance of these very complex mixtures can change drastically, resulting in lack of uniformity and possibly coarse-textured open turf subject to weed invasion, more frequent mowing and increased susceptibility to disease. Too many grasses in one mixture is also economically wrong and wastes money.

Choice of mixture must be governed by the type of lawn required and the availability of suitable grasses for local soils and conditions.

Is the soil usually dry or moist; is it of heavy, light or medium texture? What purpose is the grass to be put to – ornamental lawn, play area for children, tennis courts, or just a piece of ground for hanging the washing out? How much care is the turf likely to receive? Is ease and frequency of mowing likely to be a factor? Is the soil particularly acid or alkaline?

It is always much better to choose a mixture of grasses suited to the conditions under which they are to grow and flourish, rather than change the top soil or apply extensive application of fertilisers and top dressings.

The list below details a number of prescriptions of grass-seed mixtures for various purposes and conditions. These can be adopted to particular needs by reference to each individual species in this book, where more detail is given of the equally important characteristics of bred cultivars which usually have many advantages over the ordinary strains and often produce very vigorous plants. See Grass Breeding.

102

MIXTURES FOR SUPER-FINE LAWNS This is the type of lawn for the enthusiast who wants the best lawn in his neighbourhood. Such luxury lawns require regular routine management, will not stand up to the same prolonged hard wear as those containing rye-grass, are more expensive to establish and need more careful site preparations. Luxury type lawns must consist of fine-leaved grasses and have the ability to produce uniform growth of superb appearance and colour, offer excellent persistency even under close and frequent mowing. An ideal mixture for most soil types is:

80 per cent Chewings fescue

20 per cent brown top.

If the more bristly type of fescue turf is preferred to the leafy sward of brown top, increase the Chewings fescue content by 15 per cent at the expense of brown top.

Some lawn owners may prefer to spread their risk over three instead of only two cultivars and use a mixture composed of equal parts, by weight of:

Chewings fescue

red or creeping fescue

brown top.

Similarly, the individual grasses can be made up of one or more cultivars – again to spread the risk. 'Highlight' is an excellent Chewings fescue cultivar but could perhaps be usefully mixed with 'Waldorf' which is resistant to red thread disease (qv) and has a better summer colour, although it is less attractive in colour during the winter months.

A mixture with good resistance to drought is essential for lighter soils and low rain-fall areas and is best provided by a prescription containing a greater proportion of rhizomatous (qv) grasses and cultivars able to withstand wear:

20 per cent Chewings fescue

45 per cent red or creeping fescue

25 per cent smooth-stalked meadow-grass

10 per cent brown top.

For tennis courts or croquet lawns, cut the Chewings fescue by half, the red fescue by one third and double the smooth-stalked meadow-grass content. The resulting sward of dwarf growing, drought resistant grasses will have good texture, the ability to recover rapidly from wear and with the additional benefits of winter hardiness in temperate climates and comparative ease of management.

GOOD QUALITY LAWNS Rye-grass is excellent for lawns intended for hard use rather than ornament. Like other broad-leaved grasses, as a main constituent of turf it has an undeserved bad reputation chiefly brought about by the numerous poor and common strains which have been used in the cheaper, nondescript types of lawn mixtures. Newly bred modern cultivars are leafier and do not grow so high as the common strains; they also show greater persistency under close mowing regimes and survival after wear. Modern cultivars of rye-grass can now be seriously considered for moderately fine turf and if properly managed, can provide dual purpose sward – a sward to set off the flower border, shrubbery and house and yet at the same time stand up to the wear and tear of a play area for children.

Rye-grass and most other broad-leaved grasses grow more rapidly than the finer types; this provides the advantage of quick establishment and the disadvantage of more frequent mowing being necessary. It is less expensive than fescue and bent grasses but does not provide the appearance of a tightly knit green carpet; nor is it so easy to produce the distinct zebra stripes, so loved by many enthusiasts, when mowing or rolling an established rye-grass sward with a roller-mower. Rye-grass turf is in any case best cut with a rotary machine set no closer than $\frac{3}{4}$in in above soil level.

Any broad-leaved grass is, of course, a weed in a bent/fescue type of lawn; yet in an exclusively broad-leaved based lawn, the naturally coarse and indigenous grasses are unlikely to be noticed.

For turf which does not need excessive mowing, looks its best under constant use and keeps its colour for most of the year, use:

20 per cent perennial rye-grass

50 per cent smooth-stalked meadow-grass

10 per cent Timothy-grass

20 per cent red or creeping fescue.

A simpler and more hard wearing mixture suitable for heavy traffic like football pitches is best made with only two ingredients:

80 per cent perennial rye-grass

20 per cent crested dog's-tail.

Dense, compact and richly coloured turf for good wear and persistency can also be grown by mixing:

35 per cent perenial rye-grass

45 per cent smooth-stalked meadow-grass

20 per cent Timothy-grass.

On heavy soils use rough-stalked instead of smooth-stalked meadow-grass.

TURF FOR DIFFICULT SITUATIONS For a lawn where the soil is heavy:

20 per cent crested dog's-tail

40 per cent Chewings fescue

20 per cent brown top

20 per cent rough-stalked meadow-grass.

For lawn in dry and hot situations:

50 per cent crested dog's-tail

50 per cent smooth-stalked meadow-grass.

For lawns in damp and shady spots, particularly under trees, use wood meadow-grass which does best in situations where the ground normally remains bare or grows moss. Annual meadow-grass, unsuitable for fine turf, is a suitable substitute.

For particularly shaded situations on most types of soil use:

50 per cent rough-stalked meadow-grass

25 per cent wood meadow-grass

25 per cent fine-leaved sheep's fescue.

If the soil is inclined to be dry, acid and peaty, subsitute wavy hair-grass for the wood meadow-grass.

For lawns in cities, the mixture should always contain a good proportion of smooth-stalked meadow-grass and/or crested dog's-tail. However comprehensive, published mixtures can serve only as a guide and any reputable seedsman, given details of soil-type, situation and the purpose of the lawn is glad to advise from his experience and in the light of the many available cultivars. He is best equipped to give the correct advice on seed mixtures not only in terms of soil and location but as regards rate of growth (frequency of mowing), mode of growth (creeping or tufted), disease resistance, winter hardiness and colour. He will also be able to advise on the appropriate mixture for specific purposes.

Always choose a reputable seedsman as your supplier of grass-seed mixtures; do not be ruled by price alone as the cost of the seed is a small investment in relation to the life of the lawn and the time and hard work in making it.

Avoid all mixtures that are sold without a detailed description of the grasses they contain. Many of these 'commercial' mixtures could contain grasses quite unsuitable for the production of fine turf and some of the cheaper mixtures may contain impurities. Endeavour to always buy mixtures containing certified seeds, that is where a certifying authority, usually run under the aegis of the Government of the producing country, checks that the seeds have come from the original plants of the particular cultivar.

Certification is an important safeguard for the buyer. For climatic and economic reasons many grass-seeds are produced abroad and in this event are usually grown under an internationally recognised certification scheme.

Finally, always enquire for the purity (qv) and germination (qv) counts of the seed you are buying. No reputable seed house would refuse to give you this information which, combined with certification, are your guarantee of pure viable seeds of the cultivars of your choice.

Seedling Diseases

A number of fungi, either seed or soil-borne, may attack freshly sown seed and so prevent germination or at a later stage infect the young growing seedlings and cause their collapse. The fungi responsible are species of *Fusarium*, *Helminthosporium* and *Pythium*. Potential infection may be minimised by careful preparation of the seed bed and treating seeds, prior to sowing, with captan or thiram (qv).

See Soil Preparations and Seed Dressing.

Self-heal

Prunella vulgaris. A perennial weed usually found on heavy soils with creeping stems rooting at the nodes. It has heavily veined, oval leaves and purple flowers (Fig 38). Not difficult to kill with selective herbicides. See Weeds and Weedkillers and Appendix 3.

Senecio vulgaris See Groundsel

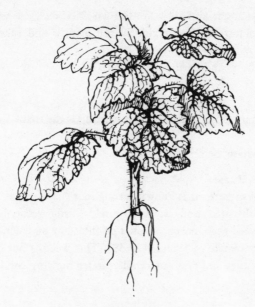

Fig 38 Self-heal

Shaded Lawns

Satisfactory turf can be grown even under these conditions although a little extra care and attention may be needed.

Soil preparation, sowing and maintenance is exactly as for any other piece of turf. But it is important to choose the correct grass seed mixture and feed the grasses fairly generously.

If the shade is produced by trees, leaves must always be raked or brushed up. This will at the same time scarify the lawn and prevent wet leaves from discolouring the turf and encouraging the risk of disease. If possible also remove the lower boughs of trees to permit a little more light and air to reach the grasses.

Use a grass seed mixture designed for shady conditions and which should be equally useful whether sown under trees or used to produce a sward shaded by buildings. Both wood meadow-grass and annual meadow-grass (qv) are suitable but should not be mown too closely, leaving at least 1-1½in of growth.

Feed generously and apply liberal quantities of top dressing every autumn after aeration.

Lack of sunlight and air is apt to turn soils sour, it is a good plan therefore to test the soil regularly for acidity and take remedial measures if necessary.

See Fertilisers and Feeding, also Soil Testing.

Sheath
The lower part of the grass leaf that surrounds the stem.

Sheep's Fescue See Fescues

Shepherd's Purse
Capsella bursa-pastoris is known throughout the world as a common weed of cultivated and waste ground. Easily recognised by its triangular seed-pods borne on an upright stem and which in turn rises from a rosette of leaves (Fig 39). This weed is not difficult to eradicate in turf and dies out rapidly under mowing conditions. See Appendix 3.

Silverweed
Potentilla anserina. This is a stoloniferous perennial weed which is

Fig 39 Shepherd's Purse

108

frequently found in turf and especially in damp situations. Its yellow flowers are set off by its fern-like leaves with silvery-hairy undersides. Repeated application of selective weedkillers are necessary to control it. See Weeds and Weedkillers and Appendix 3.

Simazine
A soil-acting herbicide used for a variety of purposes including total weed control on waste land, paths and drives. Do not plant crops on ground treated with simazine for at least seven months after application.

Slugs
There are many different species of slug some of which are known to be troublesome on lawns, particularly on newly sown turf. Suspect slug damage during warm and muggy weather if ragged leaves or a particularly thin stand of seedlings are observed.

To control them, use proprietary slug-killers in pelleted form based on methiocarb or metaldehyde.

Smooth-stalked Meadow-grass See Meadow-grass

Snow-mould
A fungal disease of turf; see Fusarium Patch.

Sodium Chlorate
Total weedkiller only suitable for use on paths and drives; an inflammable material that should be stored and used with care.

Soil-borne
Carried in the soil, usually of disease organisms.

Soil Preparation
The ideal time to establish a lawn is during spring or autumn. Preparatory work should commence at the beginning of the previous season so that a full six months may be devoted to preparation. All work must be done thoroughly and in the correct sequence, because if

any of the fundamentals are left undone or are only sketchily completed, their neglect will remain a visible reproach until they are subsequently corrected at greater expense of effort, time and money.

Many beautiful lawns have been created on sites that were once the dumping ground of builders' rubble, so do not be daunted if your site looks like a refuse patch.

First remove and store all bricks, clinker and large stones, these may well be useful later on if drainage has to be undertaken. Next examine the ground systematically and critically. If, as is likely, it supports a fine crop of weeds, dig out all the tap rooted and perennial species – such as docks, thistles and nettles very thoroughly and burn them. Now cut down the remaining vegetation as close to the ground as possible. This operation will probably expose more rubble which must be added to the original heap.

If the site is extremely rough and perennial weeds, scrub and brambles are too numerous for individual removal, destroy them with a weedkiller. Cut them down first with scythe or sickle and when the plants start to show new growing shoots and are at their most susceptible, the entire area should be sprayed with a weedkiller. Use 2,4,5-T (qv) on its own, or if woody and herbaceous weeds are present in combination with 2,4-D (qv), dalapon (qv) can also be mixed in to destroy coarse grasses. A chemical named paraquat (qv) is more useful for the less woody-stemmed weeds, but it does control a wide range of annual broad-leaved weeds and grasses very satisfactorily as well as killing the tops of perennial weeds. Always study and comply with the manufacturers' instructions and application rates when using weedkillers, their mis-use can have serious consequences.

On meadowland sites it is sufficient to skim off the grass with a spade. Stack the turves, grass side downwards, as they will gradually rot and provide useful compost for later use.

Old and offending tree stumps (qv) should be removed. The overall ground level will now be apparent and inspection of it may well reveal areas of subsoil that were thrown up during house-building operations. Subsoil will not sustain vigorous plant growth and because of this must be removed by digging or skimming off with a spade. Failure to do this will inevitably result in a poor sward of uneven texture and growth. Alternatively, if there is much of this subsoil and its removal would prove to be too big an operation, it can be roughly levelled off and the whole area covered with top soil, purchased from a nurseryman, to a depth of at least six inches. See Drainage and Levelling.

SOIL CONDITIONS AND THEIR IMPROVEMENT The size of the lawn-to-be will determine whether it is to be dug by hand or worked by mechanical means such as a rotovator or even small plough obtainable through a local contractor. Do not work the soil if it is wet, as this will harm its structure. Look out for pests when the soil is being prepared – slugs, ants, wood lice, chafer grubs, leatherjackets – all should be destroyed (qv). Whichever tool is used, cultivation must be at least nine inches deep (the depth of an average spade blade) if the top soil extends to that depth. If it does not, depth of cultivation must not exceed the depth of top soil, otherwise the sub soil will be brought to the surface.

A fork, when working heavy soil, makes for easier work than a spade. Employ the trench method of digging (qv) and break the surface of the sub soil before turning the next top spit on to it. Any large stones, creeping underground stems of couch grass, or creeping thistle or bindweed must be removed. Annual weeds can be dug in and will add humus-forming material. This is the moment to introduce the correct soil conditioners, if the millions of comparatively short rooted grasses are to flourish. Once the lawn is planted and growing it will be too late, and correction will then only be possible by means of expensive and constant top dressing.

The ideal soil has a loamy texture, contains humus, is well drained and possesses sufficient plant food to encourage and maintain growth. Unfortunately not many soils have all these attributes naturally. Nutrient deficiences can be quickly and accurately determined by the use of one of the inexpensive kits now on the market, making it possible to analyse the soil and correct its wants. See Soil Testing.

Soil texture and its deficiences will soon become apparent on working the soil. A good method of testing is to rub a little moist soil between fore-finger and thumb. Clay is sticky when wet; it has a smooth feel and polished appearance. Light soils feel rough as a

111

result of their high sand content and crumble easily. Loam feels neither sticky nor rough, but has the smooth feel of clay without its plastic qualities. Peat and chalk soils are of course, visually recognised by their respective high chalk and fibre content.

HEAVY SOILS These soils usually contain clay and are potentially rich in plant food but lack porosity; they benefit by the incorporation of such coarse materials as lime free sand dug in at the rate of roughly 10-14lb per sq yd. Coke-breeze, ashes, grit and road sweepings are also good. Moistened coarse baled peat (qv), applied as a layer 2-3in deep and then forked into the surface, not only improves the soil structure but also provides a source of valuable organic material. Leaf mould and well-rotted garden compost perform the same function. Lime or gypsum (sulphate of lime) applications are often advocated for the breaking up of stiff clay soils, but should not be applied indiscriminately and certainly not without first analysing the soil for its pH value (qv).

LIGHT SOILS These are made up of sand and grit particles, lose their moisture quickly, and are liable to have their nutrients leached out with the drainage water. They lack organic, moisture-holding material. Well-rotted farmyard manure at the rate of approximately 10-15cwt per 100sq yd is the ideal treatment. Failing that, the best alternatives are well-rotted garden refuse, dried sewage, hop manure or 7-10lb of moistened peat per sq yd. Light soils are hungry soils and the danger of giving them too much organic matter is non-existent. Excellent, although rarely possible in practice, is the addition of clay at the rate of 15-20cwt per 100 sq yd. This should be evenly distributed, left for the winter frosts and rains to break up, and worked in during the spring.

CHALK SOILS These are usually shallow in depth and, like light soils, need much humus-forming matter. Stones and flints are often profuse and the largest should be removed. The smaller ones should disappear beneath a succession of top dressings. The breaking up of the solid chalk below the top soil level is a laborious task but will be amply repaid by a quite startling improvement of growth. The soil should be tested for pH value and excess alkalinity be corrected with applications of either peat or sulphate of ammonia.

PEAT SOILS These usually suffer from poor drainage and acidity. The latter can be corrected by liming during autumn or winter. Lime should always be applied either as ground chalk or ground limestone, from 2 to 6oz per sq yd according to the pH value. See Drainage.

LOAM This is the ideal soil, midway between light and heavy, easily workable, retains moisture and makes the most of any humus-forming matter that is added during cultivation.

Lime is an important constituent of most fertile soils and by its absence or presence determines acidity or alkalinity and also contributes to porosity of soils. As a conditioner it should be introduced into the soil before the lawn is sown or turfed.

GOOD FOUNDATIONS Having completed the work of drainage, made good the deficiences revealed by soil analysis, and roughly levelled off the site, the ground must now be left to settle for at least a week or two before the final levelling and seed bed preparation can be undertaken. Timing must, however, be considered first. If it is autumn and the soil is already wet, with danger of night frosts cutting down the freshly germinating grass, do not embark on the final stages of preparation. It is better to let the winter rains, snow and frost work on the roughly dug area. If it is still early summer however, the final levelling and seeding can be safely undertaken, though it is even better to complete the work of levelling and then allow the site to lie fallow until sowing during early autumn. This will allow the weed seeds to germinate during the summer months, they can then be raked and hoed at two or three-weekly intervals, this will also aerate the soil while the ground is firmed by treading. Only attempt this in dry soil, or the vital crumb structure will be impaired.

On very weedy ground, particularly if it contains much couch grass, it may be better to grow a crop of an early maturing cultivar of potatoes rather than permit the ground to lie fallow. The normal earthing up of potatoes exposes a bigger surface area of soil for weeds to germinate in and regular hoeing will benefit crumb structure and keep the young weeds in check. The further forking when the potatoes are harvested during mid-summer will again aerate the soil and at the same time enable all weed roots to be removed. If a generous dressing of fertiliser was applied prior to the planting of potatoes there will be considerable residual nutrients left in the soil to benefit the young grasses.

In lighter soils, better than a potato crop to check the weed problem is green manuring as this increases the humus content. Mustard is the seed usually chosen, because of its rapid growth. Mustard may be sown at any time between early spring and late summer at the rate of $\frac{1}{8}$–$\frac{1}{4}$oz of seed per sq yd. The crop is dug in just before it flowers, together with all but the most pernicious weeds, which should be removed and burnt.

GETTING READY TO SOW, PLANT OR TURF (QV) With the soil in good fertile condition and the final levels already established, raking and slow rolling must now be carried out alternately over the whole area, with every operation made in a different direction each time. Stones, twigs and large fractions of heavy soil, if still present, must be removed, the aim being that no particle left should be larger than a pea. Further consolidation by walking over the ground in short steps putting full weight on the heels, will add the final touch, and also break up the last remaining particles of soil.

A fine tilth is essential for seeded lawns. If turf is to be laid or tufts planted, it is not quite so important, but even so preparations should not be skimped, for the soil must be friable for the grasses to root into the deeper layers.

The last and final step prior to planting is the application of a pre-seeding fertiliser (qv). See Drainage, Levelling, Sowing, Turfing and Planting.

Soil Testing

Turf cannot flourish unless there is food in the soil, properly balanced food, that is, of the right kind. Like all vegetation, turf requires the three major plant foods, nitrogen, phosphate and potash (qv) together with the correct level of acidity or alkalinity.

To plan a balanced and economical programme to maintain soil fertility it is essential to know what, if anything, the soil lacks, or whether it has an excess of any major plant food.

Either professional advice can be obtained which is usually expensive, or one of the readily available soil testing kits bought. These consist of a number of chemicals which are mixed with soil samples taken from various parts of the area to be tested.

Individual tests for each major plant food and acidity produce a colour reaction, the colour is then matched with one on the colour chart provided and which not only defines the percentage of deficiency but advises on the type and quality of fertiliser to be used for correction.

Soil Types See Soil Preparation

Sorrel

Common sorrel *(Rumex acetosa)* and Sheep's sorrel *(R. acetosella)* are weeds, with the former usually found on moist, neutral soils and the latter on drier, lighter and more acid land.

The tips of the arrow-shaped leaves of common sorrel tend to turn inwards to the smooth, hair-less stem; whilst the leaves of sheep's sorrel are much narrower and have more defined lobes positioned at right angles to the leaf.

The flowers of both species turn red when nearing maturity. Can be controlled with selective weedkillers. See Weeds and Weedkillers and Appendix 3.

Sour Soil

Another term to describe the acidity of soils. See Lime, pH, and Soil Testing.

Sowing

SEED REQUIREMENTS Buy sufficient seed to sow at the rate of 1½oz per sq yd. If less is sown, the grass is apt to be thin and sparse and if seed is applied at a higher rate, the too-crowded seedlings may be subject to 'damping off' (qv). When total seed requirements have been calculated, round the figure up to the nearest pound and buy a little extra for reseeding thin patches or repairing damaged areas later.

BEST TIME TO SOW Sow in spring or autumn but remember it is always unwise to hurry. Wait a few days if necessary and make sure the seedbed is fine and fit for sowing. Test it by walking across it – if the soil sticks to the shoes delay sowing until drier conditions prevail.

Early autumn is the best time for sowing as the ground is warm from the summer sun and chances of natural moisture are much greater than during the spring. Weed competition is apt to be stronger with spring sowings, and if the following summer is dry, the seedlings may have to be watered.

SEED PREPARATION PRIOR TO SOWING Different grasses bear seeds of varying weights and sizes which segregate in the bag during the course of handling and delivery. Mix the seeds thoroughly by shaking the bag, or if the quantity is too large, with a spade on a previously swept floor and which is under cover. Grass seeds are light and even a moderate wind is apt to blow them away, while an unswept floor may harbour weed seeds.

Weigh one portion of the 1½oz required per sq yd to ascertain its volume, this varies according to the seed mixture chosen. Find a suitable container to hold this small quantity of seed so that it can be used as a measure during sowing, rather than continue weighing each portion. It may be a heaped soupspoonful or perhaps just fit into an empty ice cream carton.

GROUND PREPARATION Divide the area into one yard squares by placing string across it in both directions. Another and less complicated method is to use a one-yard-square template preferably made from thick gauge wire or bamboo canes lashed together and move this along the ground as sowing progresses (Fig 40).

SOWING Choose a wind free day and apply the seed from the volume measure to every one of the marked out square yards. To avoid

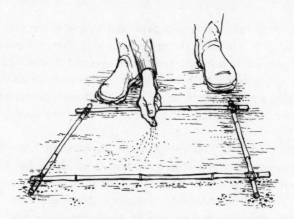

Fig 40 Sowing seed with the aid of a one yard square template

116

uneven growth make sure that the seed is evenly distributed and right into the corners outlined by the string or template.

Many gardeners are a little apprehensive of sowing lawn seed but after completing the first ten square yards or so in orthodox fashion, confidence grows. At this point fill a cupped hand with a volume measure full of seed, close the hand and move it to a position some nine or twelve inches above the ground. It may be, depending on the mixture being used, that only part of the amount of seed needed per square yard can be held. No matter, take two handfuls per square yard and with a circular motion of the fingers let the seed dribble on to the marked out area from between the fingers. This method is easier and more even seed distribution is obtained than by scattering from a container.

If there is a large lawn to sow, a mechanical distributor (see lawn spreader) speeds and eases some of the work. It is a two-wheeled machine, connected by a container fitted with interchangeable rollers each with different sized indentations. The container, prior to being filled with seed, is fitted with the roller designed to distribute $1\frac{1}{2}$oz of seed per sq yd and the machine is pushed across the ground surface similarly to a lawn mower. The same machine fitted with differently indented rollers can also be used for applying fertiliser and dressings to lawns.

Irrespective of the sowing method used, splitting the seed to be sown into two equal portions and sowing each half separately and in opposite directions aids more even distribution. An alternative to achieve the same end is to increase the bulk to be sown by mixing the seed with four times its own weight of sharp sand prior to sowing.

Immediately after sowing, and in an attempt to cover the seeds, lightly rake the ground in two directions at right angles to each other. Use a light rake so that those seeds that are covered are only just below the soil surface. Many of them will be left exposed, but this is unavoidable and most of them will contribute to the lawn.

Rolling the freshly seeded ground is often advocated but seed establishment will be very much better if the temptation is resisted. Rolled ground puddles after heavys rain and subsequently cracks when dry conditions return. The slightly ridged surface left by the rake also prevents light soil from blowing.

PROTECTION FROM BIRDS If the seed was not treated with a bird repellent preparation, adequate protection for the smaller lawn is easily provided by stringing black cotton 2-3in above the surface. Be sure it is taken up before the first mowing to prevent the cotton from twisting round the cutting cylinder of the mower. Larger areas are better protected by suspending old fruit or soup cans from stout string supported across the areas. Tear off the labels first as birds usually shy away from glittering surfaces. If this has no effect, try putting a marble or pebble in the can; the slightest breeze makes the marble roll inside and the resultant noise disturbs the birds.

GERMINATION AND WATERING The finer the mixture the longer it will take to emerge. Rye grasses will show green within 10 to 14 days from sowing, fescues and bents may take up to 21 days or even one month. If the ground has been well prepared, watering is not necessary. The seed, if adequately protected against birds, will lie in the ground quite happily and in a dormant state until moisture is available to trigger germination. Autumn sowing rarely presents drought problems, but spring-sown seeds can reach a critical stage if drought follows rain soon after sowing. The moisture provided by the rain may have been only just sufficient to start the process of germination, and the young seedlings can be severely damaged by dry conditions at that time. In such circumstances watering is essential. Never water unless you do so copiously to moisten the ground to a depth of three inches. Use a sprinkler, as a hose is inclined to wash the seeds from the soil.

MOWING THE NEW LAWN The germinating grasses tend to lift the soil as they push through the surface, and this should be corrected by a light rolling when they are 1in high and before the first cut takes place. The back roller of a lawn mower is quite heavy enough; roll also even if a side wheel machine is used for in addition to consolidating the surface, rolling encourages the grass to produce additional side shoots. When the grass is 1½in to 2in high, usually from four to six weeks after sowing, it is ready for the first topping. Do not attempt to cut the grass close and only remove the top of the blades; succeeding cuts are dependent on the speed of growth and should be timed to keep the grass at a constant height of ¾in. Take great care when turning the mower so that the seedlings are not bruised or torn from the ground. In the case of autumn-sown lawns, the weather may allow no more than one or two cuts. If weather is mild and growth continues, treat as lawns planted in spring, but cut no lower than ¾in until the following year.

WEEDS However well the ground has been prepared, weeds are certain to emerge with the grass. They are naturally present in the ground and the ideal seed bed conditions prepared for the lawn seed also favour the weed seeds. As they are likely to be mostly annuals they disappear with continual mowings. If perennial weeds, couch or other weed grasses are present, dig them out immediately, making sure all their roots are removed. Level and consolidate the soil to fit in with the surrounding area and sprinkle seed on the surface. The resulting scar, glaring at first, soon greens over to match the lawn.

If the weed problem is severe, use one of the specialised weedkillers designed for freshly sown turf.

Speedwells
Two of the several species are troublesome weeds in turf.

Thyme-leaved speedwell *(Veronica serpyllifolia)* is a perennial with short creeping stems, pale green oval leaves and white to pale blue flowers. Application of lawn sand provides quite effective control especially if combined with raking.

Wall speedwell *(V. arvensis)* is an annual weed usually of prostrate habit when found in fine-textured turf. Unlike thyme-leaved speedwell it thrives on the lighter and drier soils and is easily recognised by its triangular, heavily toothed leaves. It can be checked by weedkillers. See Weeds and Weedkillers and Appendix 3.

Spergula arvensis See Spurrey

Spiking See Aeration

Sports Turf Research Institute
An institute of worldwide reputation, founded in 1929 and situated at Bingley, Yorkshire, England. The institute carries out valuable work in all spheres of turf culture, from scientific studies of a whole host of individual problems to the evaluation of turf-grass cultivars,

pesticides and machinery used for sward management. Reports on these and other turf topics are published regularly in the Institute's quarterly bulletin and annual journal.

It runs courses for groundsmen, organises lectures throughout the United Kingdom, issues a quarterly magazine and conducts an efficient advisory service for the construction and maintenance of private and public sports grounds on a membership basis. Most of these services are also available to private individuals.

Spurrey
Spergula arvensis. An annual weed also known as corn spurrey and which soon disappears from turf as a result of regular mowing. The plant is somewhat sticky and has very narrow leaves which grow in whorls. It has small white flowers.

Squitch See Couch

Stolon
A lateral stem creeping along the surface of the ground, rooting at the nodes, and there forming leaf and root growth (Fig 41). Example: *Agrostis stolonifera* (creeping bent).

Storksbill
Erodium cicutarium. A tap-rooted plant usually found on light sandy

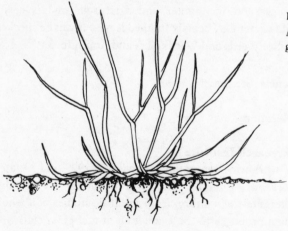

Fig 41
A stoloniferous grass

soils; easily recognised by its fern-like, rather prostrate leaves and purple-pink flowers. Can be checked with selective herbicides. See Weeds and Weedkillers and Appendix 3.

Sulphate of Ammonia
Also known as ammonium sulphate it is a useful nitrogenous turf fertiliser and combined with iron sulphate is a constituent of lawn sand. Never apply more than $\frac{1}{2}$oz per sq yd at any one time, but repeated applications up to a maximum of four at monthly intervals during the height of the growing season are beneficial. Sulphate of ammonia increases the acidity of soils and also kills some weeds.

Sulphate of Iron
Also known as green vitriol or ferrous sulphate. A very useful material for a variety of purposes in turf production and maintenance and which with the exception of being used alone for the control of algae and lichens (qv) is usually combined with other chemicals for optimum efficiency. It is a constituent of lawn sand and so has a stimulating effect on grasses but also kills some weeds and mosses; it lowers the alkalinity of soils and acts as a fungicide for the control of fairy rings. May also be used as a temporary measure to control fusarium patch. (qv)

Sulphate of Lime See Gypsum

Sulphate of Potash
The most suitable of potassic fertilisers for lawns and also for mixing with nitrogenous and phosphate fertilisers to form compounds. See Potash.

Superphosphate
A phosphatic fertiliser available in powder and granular form. Usually applied in combination with nitrogen and potash (qv). See Phosphate.

Systemic Chemicals
A chemical (insecticide or fungicide) which when applied to foliage is

absorbed, enters the sap stream and is translocated to other parts of the plant. It is consequently more persistent than a contact chemical which only adheres to and acts on the surface of the plant.

Take All
Ophiobolus graminis also known as ophiobolus patch (qv); a fungal disease of fine turf.

Taraxacum officinale See Dandelion

Thatch See Matted Turf

Thiabendazole
A systemic fungicide for the control of fusarium patch (qv) and other diseases of fine turf.

Thiram
A fungicide used as a seed dressing (qv) to control seedling diseases (qv); also partially protects newly sown seeds from being eaten by birds. Apply 50 per cent thiram seed dressing at 1½oz per 28lb. Thiram is a skin irritant.

Thistle
Selective weedkillers are well able to control thistles which occasionally invade turf. Usually two species are responsible, either creeping thistle *(Cirsium arvense)* or stemless thistle *(C. acaulon)*. The latter also known as ground thistle, has hairs on the underside of the rosette forming leaves which hug the ground. The creeping thistle has a more upright habit of growth, white creeping roots and very spiny leaves. See Weeds and Weedkillers and also Appendix 3.

Thrift See Sea Pink

Thyme
Thymus. A dwarf growing plant capable of producing aromatic and colourful swards which require little or no mowing. See Grass Substitutes.

Thymus See Thyme and Grass Substitutes

Tiller
A shoot emerging from the base of a plant.

Timothy-grass

Phleum pratense also known as cat's-tail. A hard wearing, somewhat coarse, stoloniferous perennial for moist situations on heavy soils. Only fit for the second class, less closely cut lawn (Fig 42).

'Aberystwyth S50' Timothy-grass was bred at the Welsh Plant Breeding Station in the United Kingdom and used in the mixture for sowing the Munich Stadium for the Olympic Games. It is persistent, able to withstand hard wear, drought tolerant and winter hardy.

'Aberystwyth S48' Timothy-grass is similar to 'S50' but blends less well with fescues and bents because of its larger leaves and blue-green colour.

'Bariton' is very hard wearing, has good winter colour and withstands medium height cutting conditions.

Ligule

Fig 42 Timothy-grass

Top Dressing

Application of fertilisers, especially if mixed with a carrier such as peat or sand, are often referred to as top dressing although the more usual and correct interpretation of the term is the application of bulky organic and other materials to the surface of the lawn and preferably after aeration (qv). Top dressings improve the soil structure, level minor depressions, help drainage of heavy soils and increase the water-holding capacity of light soils. Repeated applications over the years improve the condition of the grass and produce springy, resilient turf.

Top dressings can consist of any materials normally used to improve the condition of soils and are best applied during autumn or early winter for rain to wash them into the soil. An average mixture consists of two parts coarse sand, four parts loam and one part granulated peat, all parts by volume. Add autumn fertiliser to the heap and mix the materials well.

On very heavy soils, the sand content can be beneficially increased at the expense of loam. Other materials for top dressing are very useful; for example, a mixture of equal portions of good friable top soil mixed with an equal quantity of peat, adding coarse sand or coke breeze to alleviate heavy soils, or if loam is difficult to obtain, use 2 parts peat and 1 part sand for light soils and 1 part peat and 2 parts sand for heavy ground. Even a good sized bucket full of peat for every square yard makes a wonderful difference to the condition of the turf. If the mixture contains any large particles, sieve it through $\frac{1}{4}$in mesh before applying it at the rate of 2-3lb per sq yd. A shovel full equals approximately the right amount per sq yd and is a handy tool for scattering the material. Rake or brush the top dressing well into the turf to make it penetrate into the previously spiked holes. Brushing also helps to level depressions and prevents the grass from being smothered.

Deeper hollows are similarly corrected but to avoid burying the grass, they should be built up by a succession of dressings rather than one heavy application at any one time.

Aeration by spiking naturally aids top dressing to penetrate more quickly and efficiently, but if it is not possible to carry out this somewhat laborious task, top dressing brushed well into the turf stimulates the grass tremendously and is certainly worth both the expense and effort involved.

Trace Elements
Chemical elements usually present in the soil, and which are essential to plant life although taken up in only minute amounts. Some of the principal trace elements are: boron, copper, iron, manganese and zinc.

Trees
The smaller types of ornamental trees and shrubs are unlikely to compete with the turf growing beneath them. Establishment and maintenance of turf right up to the bole of large, mature and specimen trees is more difficult as the grass is likely to lack sunshine and moisture and yet is subject to the sometimes heavy and constant drip of water from trees during the winter months.

The problem may be solved in one of two ways. Grow no turf around the tree, and establish shade tolerant ground cover plants, or alternatively, work and enrich the soil at the base of the tree and sow wood meadow-grass or annual meadow-grass or a mixture of both. Both grasses tolerate deciduous tree shade but to make the best of them never cut them as close as the remainder of the turf, leaving at least 1-1½in of growth. Otherwise treat these areas exactly as the lawn surrounding them. Do, however, be careful to avoid possible damage if using selective weedkillers.

Tree Stumps
When felling trees, do not make the mistake of cutting the trunk too close to the ground but leave at least 3ft to 4ft above soil level. It is easy then to stretch rope between the trunk and a powered vehicle and pull the stump, with most of the roots, from the ground. If old and offending tree stumps are the problem, they are easily dealt with during soil preparation and can either be dug out or burnt by lighting a fire round their base.

Another often successful means of disposing of tree stumps is to drill vertical holes, 1in in diameter 6in deep and 12in apart all over the stump. Fill the holes with saltpetre (potassium nitrate), top up with water and seal the holes with waterproof tape or putty. After three to four months, open the holes, fill with paraffin and ignite. The stump should burn itself out slowly.

Applications of one of the many brush-wood killers are quite effective as are ammonium sulphamate crystals which contain nitrogen and so hasten the destruction of the stump. Dissolve 1lb of the crystals in 1gal of water and paint all cut surfaces as well as the bark above ground level, making sure you give a good coating to the exposed horizontal section of the bark along the stump periphery.

Do not neglect to remove all roots from the soil as these, if left to rot in the ground, can be a source of fungal growth on the surface of the lawn.

Chemical treatment is unfortunately not always successful with very big stumps and may have to be repeated more than once. Many old stumps can make attractive features on a lawn if suitably clothed with a variety of climbing plants planted at their base.

Trifolium dubium See Clover

Trifolium repens See Clover and Grass Substitutes

Trulute
A tool used for the even distribution of top dressing.

Turfing
Turfing is not a difficult task, rather easier than seeding, and gives tremendous satisfaction as turf by turf the green expanse rapidly increases to form a lawn. The ground must be adequately prepared, as for seeding, and delivery and laying of the turves carefully timed and organised to prevent them from deteriorating during prolonged storage.

WHEN TO LAY TURVES The cool conditions during both late autumn and early spring provide the optimum chance of establishment; turves are not then liable to parch and crack under a hot sun and have ample natural moisture to help extend their root system. Turfing can continue throughout the winter months provided the

126

ground is free from frost and not too wet to work.

NUMBER OF TURVES REQUIRED To calculate the number of 3ft by 1ft turves required first ascertain the size of the area to be turfed in square feet and divide by three; for example, an area of 30ft by 30ft requires 300 turves to cover it.

DELIVERY OF TURVES Do not give the order to deliver until the ground is completely ready as turves quickly lose quality on being stored and must be laid promptly. Turves are heavy and to save the work and deterioration which takes place on extra handling, have them unloaded as near the site as possible.

There is no objection to stacking them to a maximum height of three feet provided they can be used within two or three days. When stacking, leave plenty of air vents in the stack to avoid heating. If this proves impossible, or they cannot be dealt with quickly enough, spread them out singly on vacant and preferably shaded ground, grass side uppermost. The turves may be delivered in rolls, if so, unroll them first. Intervening frost causes no damage but protection with a plastic sheet, to save the turves from the worst of drying winds and heavy rains, is beneficial.

TURF EXAMINATION Before placing each turf in its final position examine it carefully for weeds and the evenness of its depth. Correction, if needed, is best carried out at this early stage rather than in the finished lawn.

Weeds or coarse grasses are easily removed by simultaneously pulling the weed leaves from one side of the turf and pressing the roots through from underneath.

Turves of uneven depth spoil the lawn level and have to be 'boxed'. Construct a wooden frame of the same internal dimensions as the size of the turves. The depth of the frame from 1in to $1\frac{1}{2}$in decides the thickness of the turves. Set the turf, grass downwards, on to a level board and fit the frame over it. Place a long bladed knife firmly on the frame top and push it from one end to the other, slicing off excess soil and grass roots that rise above it (Fig 43).

Correction of the odd turves which are too thin is best done by packing fine soil underneath them as they are being laid.

LAYING TURVES Put the garden line in position along one of the lawn boundaries and at one end of it place one turf with its 3ft length

Fig 43 Boxing turf for trimming

parallel to the line. Then continue and lay the whole row, making sure that each turf fits closely to its neighbour to avoid unsightly gaps and ensure that they grow together quickly.

Unless the side of the lawn is exactly divisible by 3ft a strip at the end is likely to be left uncovered. A narrow strip cut from a turf and fitted at the edge dries out quickly and spoils the appearance of the lawn, instead, stop laying turves four or five feet away from the far edge. Now commence working from there in the opposite direction so that the offending gap is more centrally placed; then cut a turf to size and drop it into place (Fig 44).

To obtain maximum bonding start the second row with half a turf so that all joints are crossed like those in a brick wall.

Always work facing the ground ready to receive the turf, particularly when wet, and protect the newly laid grass with a plank. It prevents footmarks and helps consolidation. To make sure that turves are well bonded to the soil below, beat them with the back of a spade. A turf beater is an alternative tool and consists of a heavy block of wood 18in x 12in x 2in fitted with an upright broom handle. It is quickly constructed and compacts the turf well as it is systematically, but gently stamped across the surface. Avoid excessive beating which only injures the grasses. If settlement does occur it is best corrected later by application of top dressing.

128

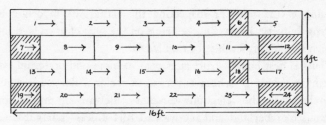

Fig 44 Turf-laying, following the numbered order and arrowed direction, cutting only shaded turves

FILLING THE GAPS However well the turves are fitted together, small gaps will be apparent where they join each other. They are quickly filled with a mixture of equal parts of sifted soil, sharp sand and peat (two spades full per sq yd) brushed over the apertures with a besom or any other stiff bristled brush.

ROLLING On the smaller lawns, particularly if the turf has been well consolidated, rolling may not be necessary. A light roller can be beneficial, but it should not be heavier than 1 hundredweight. A heavy motor mower with a good back roller provides a useful substitute.

Roll only when the turf is just moist, not wet. Watch for turves which lift during frost and re-consolidate into position as soon as ground conditions permit.

WATERING Watering is only necessary if quite exceptionally dry conditions follow spring turfing and cracks show on the surface, then, water well and preferably with a sprinkler as a hose is inclined to wash out the top dressing from between the turves.

UPKEEP Do not mow until fresh growth is showing. Unlike newly seeded lawns it is safe to take a closer cut but leave more top growth than is customary on an established lawn in order to shelter young turves from the vagaries of their first summer in new quarters.

Weedkillers should not be used until the turves are well knitted together and only after at least one cut has been taken. It is, however, beneficial to spot treat weeds as they appear, by direct application of the weedkiller to the leaves of weeds with an ordinary paint brush.

Turf Purchasing
Always buy good quality, weedfree, mature turf and insist on having

a sample turf sent, or inspecting the actual site of origin before taking delivery. Everything depends on the type of grasses in the turf which should, preferably, be fine-leaved.

Turf is best bought from sites near at hand and preferably from a specialist, many of whom advertise in regional newspapers and are also listed in the telephone directory. Beware of purchasing the famous Cumberland and sea-washed turf unless your garden has a similar environment to that whence these well-known and expensive types of turf originate, otherwise money will have been wasted as the turf will not acclimatise and is likely to degenerate over a comparatively short period.

Always make sure if delivery of the turf is included in the price; turves of about $1\frac{1}{2}$in thickness are heavy, making transport costly.

Recent new developments in turf production can substantially reduce the cost of transport, but more important, they enable the purchaser to select the cultivars from which the turf is grown. This type of turf is hydroponically produced by a growth floatation process which permits uniform carpets of purpose-seeded grass mixtures to be grown to order. Some specialists provide this service and grow the seed mixtures (qv) chosen on a thin polyether foam which in turn is floated on a liquid solution of nutrients.

Turf produced in this way is about one third of the weight of conventional turf and like a carpet, is unrolled over the ground.

Soil preparation (qv) and long term care and maintenance are the same as for conventionally established swards.

Twitch See Couch

2,4-D
A useful selective weedkiller for the control of numerous annual and perennial weeds on lawns. Available either alone or in mixtures with fenoprop, dichlorprop and mecoprop under a variety of proprietary names. Being mixed with other chemicals increases the number of different weeds controlled with only one application. Harmful to fish. 2,4-D is often combined with 2,4,5-T for use as an efficient brushwood killer (qv).

See Weeds and Weedkillers and Appendix 3.

130

2,4,5-T

A selective herbicide principally used to control tough woody weeds such as bramble and briars as well as nettles and thistles. It is even more effective and also acts on a wider range of weeds, if combined with 2,4-D. The mixture is offered under a variety of trade names. See Brushwood Killer, Weeds and Weedkillers and Appendix 3.

Urtica species See Nettles

Vegetative Reproduction

Asexual reproduction in plants achieved by first detaching and then planting a part of the parent plant. See Planting a Lawn.

Veronica species See Speedwells

Velvet Bent See Bent Grasses

Verges

The width of verges should be aimed at the traffic they are likely to have to bear; never narrower than 30in and often wider. Construction and maintenance follows that of a lawn except that verges have a much higher proportion of time-consuming edges to be maintained.

Watering

The preparation of the soil, prior to sowing, the application of top dressings, and the height at which the grass is cut, all contribute to moisture preservation. Even then, artificial watering is necessary during prolonged dry spells, as the shallow rooted grasses die without moisture supply.

Commence to water as soon as the grass loses its usual resilience and its limp leaves begin to droop. Do not wait until the ground is hard baked and the grass changes colour; some of it may already be dead, and the water is more likely to run off the hard ground instead of sinking into it. If watering is necessary, water well to moisten the soil to a depth of at least three inches. A mere sprinkling with a watering can does more damage than good; at best it only moistens the surface layer of the soil and the grass roots in search of it, travel nearer the sun's hot rays. Use a hose with a sprinkler which produces fine droplets of water to achieve more rapid penetration, or one of the perforated plastic hoses which are excellent for lawns and also easily moved about. There are a number of other automatic watering devices on the market, some of which adjust to various spray patterns for both large and small areas.

During the growing season, every sq yd of turf transpires $4\frac{1}{2}$gal of water per week. To replace this amount is equivalent to just a little less than 1in of rain. Never apply less than $2\frac{1}{2}$gal of water per sq yd at one watering and during prolonged drought do so twice weekly.

The water output of a sprinkler can be measured by placing receptacles, preferably straight sided, within the spray area. When they contain water to a depth of $\frac{1}{2}$in the lawn has received $2\frac{1}{2}$gal of water per sq yd.

Water during late afternoon or evening, and preferably when the sun is not shining on the lawn as transpiration is at its slowest then and watering achieves maximum benefit.

Waterlogging
Usually caused by consolidation and bad drainage. Spike the lawn really well, preferably with a hollow-tined fork, and brush sharp sand into the holes. If the trouble persists install drains. See Aeration and Drainage.

Wavy Hair-grass
Deschampsia flexuosa. A tufted perennial with rolled, bristle like leaves suitable for light, acid, dry soils particularly in open woodland. Ideal for establishment of turf on peat and heathland (Fig 45).

If permitted to grow without being cut, this grass produces an especially beautiful flower-head eminently suitable for dried flower arrangements.

Weeds and Weedkillers
Unless closely controlled, weeds can very soon spoil a lawn and even the presence of only a few can mar the impression of otherwise immaculate turf.

132

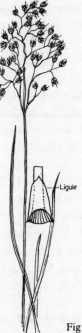

Fig 45 Wavy Hair-grass

Lawn weeds fall into two broad categories:

ANNUAL WEEDS These cause comparatively little trouble, for although they will flourish and germinate with the grass seeds on newly sown lawns they are soon killed when regular mowing begins.

PERENNIAL WEEDS A group of weeds which show greater persistency and so provide one good reason for permitting the soil to lie fallow prior to sowing with grass seeds. (See Soil Preparation.) The fallow period allows perennial and other weeds to germinate and be destroyed and thus provides less competition for the later-sown grass seeds.

Even if perennial weeds continue to appear on new or established turf, they can be controlled satisfactorily with hormone or selective weedkillers. These are selective in the sense of being able to kill broad-leaved weeds without harming the narrower leaved grasses. Individual species of weeds show more or less differing susceptibilities to the various selective herbicides available on the market for the destruction of weeds in turf. Some persistent weeds require repeated treatments before they succumb, whilst others are best dealt with by using a mixture of two herbicides. See Appendix 3 for weed table and appropriate treatments.

APPLICATION OF WEEDKILLERS Apply a light fertiliser dressing some four days before using weedkillers to encourage not only the grasses to grow but also the weeds. Well fed weeds present a larger leaf area for the weedkiller to act on with consequently improved results; the fertiliser also helps the grasses to recover more quickly from the slight check they suffer after herbicide applications.

Lawns should not be mown between fertiliser and weedkiller application, nor should they be cut for at least 48 hours afterwards as the chemicals must be permitted to do their work.

Apply weedkiller when the soil is moist and choose a calm, wind free day for applications especially if the material is in dry and powdered form. No previous fertiliser applications are necessary if a dry weedkiller/fertiliser mixture is used. These are most conveniently applied with one of the many excellent mechanical and inexpensive spreaders readily available.

Liquid weedkillers can be applied with a 2 gallon watering can fitted with a fine rose or a sprinkle bar. Be careful to apply the weedkiller to the grassed area only, and do not permit spray to drift on to neighbouring plants as they, like the weeds, can also be killed. With the can held so that the bar is 2in or so above ground level, walk up and down the lawn so that every square inch is covered with a light spray. Use a knapsack or wheel-pump sprayer for larger areas. Another, but only recently introduced, liquid weedkiller (and fertiliser) applicator, minimises the danger of fine droplets of chemical drifting on to adjoining borders. This simple, hand-propelled machine consists of a plastic tank (containing the weedkiller solution) mounted above a ribbed roller. Tank and roller are connected by a tube which meters liquid on to the ribs of the roller. As the machine is either towed or pushed at normal walking pace, the roller applies the liquid to the turf. Do not allow too great a quantity of liquid to soak into any one place to avoid damaging the roots of shrubs and trees which may have spread from adjacent beds underneath the lawn surface (Fig 46).

Application rates and other detailed instructions are always stated

Fig 46 Applying weed-killer with the aid of a sprinkle bar

clearly on the outside of chemical containers and should be observed closely, particularly if mixing two or more different preparations. To gauge correctly the appropriate amount of liquid for a given area, divide the surface with canes placed on the ground.

ROTATION OF WEEDKILLERS Appendix 3 clearly shows that no single weedkiller kills all turf weeds; each chemical has a different range of weeds it can destroy. It is consequently advisable to change chemicals for successive applications and to take full advantage of their varying capabilities.

LAWN SAND A very good weedkiller consisting of a mixture of sulphate of ammonia and sulphate of iron. It is obtainable in the form of a fine powder and functions on the selective principle. When spread on turf the individual fine particles are unable to lodge on the narrower-leaved grasses but come to rest on the broader and large

135

leaves of weeds which it scorches after a day or two. Lawn sand is usually applied at the rate of 4oz per sq yd and preferably during hot, dry weather with a chance of several dry days following application. If wet weather threatens, wait as rain can quickly wash the lawn sand off the leaves.

Lawn sand applications frequently also scorch the grass which on occasions can temporarily turn black. It will however recover after a week or so to even better and stronger growth.

Mowings from lawns treated with lawn-sand (unlike those treated with hormone weedkillers) can safely be put on the compost heap.

SPOT TREATMENT If weeds are few and sparse, rather than treating the whole area, deal with them on an individual basis. Either sprinkle a little lawn sand or dry fertiliser/weedkiller on to the weed itself; or use a liquid selective weedkiller, dipping an old paintbrush into the solution and painting the weed. Alternatively use a 3in sprinkle bar.

Aerosols charged with selective weedkillers for lawns are also readily available and very handy to use for spot treatment of weeds.

NEW LAWNS Never use the ordinary selective weedkillers on newly made lawns, whether seeded or turfed, until they are at least six months old or the young grasses may suffer irreparable damage. Fortunately there now exist two herbicides designed to deal with weeds on new lawns, namely ioxynil and morfamquat. Apply exactly as other weedkillers but not before the grasses have reached the two-leaf stage; do not use ioxynil where crested dog's-tail is a constituent of the young sward.

LAWN CLIPPINGS As herbicides remain active for some time, the first cut of grass taken after the application of weedkillers should not be used for mulching nor be put on the compost heap.

FLOWERING BULBS GROWING ON LAWNS Never apply weedkiller to turf under-planted with bulbs until their broad leaves are completely wilted.

EQUIPMENT Make it an invariable rule to wash, immediately after use, all equipment used for the application of weedkillers. Use warm water and soap and rinse thoroughly. Better still, keep a specially marked or painted watering can with sprinkle bar specifically for the application of weedkillers on turf and never use it for any other job.

CAUTION Many chemicals used in turf management are poisonous and even those described as non-poisonous may be harmful if used wrongly. Before using any chemical, read the label on the container not only to ascertain the correct application rate but also to learn the safety precautions to be observed.

Welsh Plant Breeding Station
A centre for the breeding and selection of grass cultivars situated at Aberystwyth, Cardiganshire, Wales. The various grass cultivars produced there are all differentiated by numbers prefixed with the letter 'S'. Thus, 'Aberystwyth S23' for a cultivar of perennial rye-grass and similarly 'S59' and 'S50' for red fescue and Timothy-grass respectively. All these cultivars and others are fully described under the common name of the species concerned.

Wetting Agents
These are materials added to pesticides and fungicides to improve their performance by enabling them to cover sprayed vegetation with a thin film rather than individual tiny droplets. Various makes are readily available from most good garden shops.

Wheelings
Place a strip of wire netting, preferably plastic coated, on the turf to prevent spoiling the surface with wheel-tracks left by heavy loads of soil or compost being pushed across the lawn. Turf edges too, can be damaged with the barrow wheels and are best protected with a board which at the same time serves as an incline for the barrow to travel along.

White Bent See Bent Grasses.

Wood Meadow-grass See Meadow-grasses

Yarrow
Achillea millefolium. A rhizomatous perennial weed with fern-like leaves and tiny white to pink flowers in flat heads. Found on most types of soil and drought resistant (Fig 47). The selective weedkillers MCPA and 2,4-D are unlikely to control yarrow but repeated applications of mecoprop keep it in check. See Weeds and Weedkillers and Appendix 3.

137

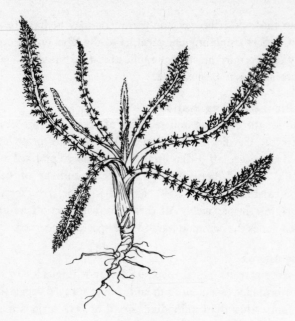

Fig 47 Yarrow

Yorkshire Fog
Holcus lanatus. A perennial grass-weed with slightly hairy grey-green leaves. Patches of Yorkshire fog in fine turf are very noticeable because of its broad leaves and light green colour. Regular raking and scarifying controls its spread. If the invasion is severe, dig out the offending patch and fill the hole with good fresh soil; then turf or re-seed. See Patching.

Appendices

Appendix 1

Principal Lawn Grasses

Annual meadow-grass	*Poa annua*
Brown top or common bent	*Agrostis tenuis*
Chewings fescue	*Festuca rubra commutata*
Cocksfoot	*Dactylis glomerata*
Creeping bent	*Agrostis stolonifera*
Crested dog's-tail	*Cynosurus cristatus*
Fine-leaved sheep's fescue	*Festuca tenuifolia*
Hard fescue	*Festuca longifolia*
Perennial rye-grass	*Lolium perenne*
Red or creeping fescue	*Festuca rubra*
Rough-stalked meadow-grass	*Poa trivialis*
Sheep's fescue	*Festuca ovina*
Smooth-stalked meadow-grass	*Poa pratensis*
Timothy-grass or cat's-tail	*Phleum pratense*
Velvet bent	*Agrostis canina*
Wavy hair-grass	*Deschampsia flexuosa*
Wood meadow-grass	*Poa nemoralis*

Appendix 2

Safety – and the Use of Garden Chemicals

Many chemicals and dressings used in turf management are poisonous and even those described as non-poisonous may be harmful if used wrongly. Before using any chemical, read the label on the container very carefully and follow the maker's recommendations meticulously in every respect. Read the label not only to ascertain the correct rate of application but also to learn the safety precautions to be observed. Keep chemicals off your skin and always wash your hands and face after use. Always keep chemicals in their original containers and never put them into drink bottles. Store them in a dry, safe place and keep them out of the reach of children.

Appendix 3

Principal Turf Weeds and Chemical Control

	MCPA only or 2,4-D	2,4-D with Fenoprop or 2,4-D with Dichlorprop	2,4-D with 2,4,5-T	Mecoprop	Mecoprop with 2,4-D	Ioxynil seedling stage only
Bird's-foot trefoil	O	X		X	X	X
Black medick	O			X	X	
Brambles			X			
Briars			X			
Buttercup, bulbous	X	X			X	X
Buttercup, creeping	X	X		X	X	X
Cat's-ear	X	X		X	X	X
Celandine, lesser	X					
Chickweeds				X	X	X
Cinquefoil	X	X			X	
Clover, white	O	X		X	X	X
Clover, yellow suckling	O	X		X	X	X
Cranesbill	O			X	X	
Crowfoot	X	X				
Daisy	X			X	X	
Dandelion	X	X			X	X
Docks, young	X			X		
Fat hen	–	–	–	–	–	–
Field wood-rush				X		
Gorse			X			
Groundsel	–	–	–	–	–	–
Heath bedstraw	X	X		X	X	
Hawk's-beard	X	X			X	
Hawkbit	X	X			X	X
Knotgrass	X			O		X
Nettles					X	X
Parsley piert				XX		
Pearlwort				X	X	
Plantain, hoary	X	X			X	X
Plantain, ribwort	X	X		X	X	X
Plantain, sea	X	X			X	X
Plantain, buck's-horn or starweed	X	X			X	X
Sea milkwort	X				X	
Sea pink	X				X	
Self-heal	X	X		X	X	
Shepherd's purse	–	–	–	–	–	–
Silverweed	X			X	X	
Speedwells				XX		X
Spurrey	–	–	–	–	–	–
Storksbill	X					
Sorrel	X	X		X	X	
Thistle	X	X	X	X	X	X
Yarrow	O	X	X	X		

Key:

O   Resistant
X   Suitable for use but, depending on the particular weed, application may have to be repeated.
XX For good control use Mecoprop mixed with Ioxynil.
–   Weeds that can be ignored on turf as regular mowing discourages them.

Appendix 4

Lawn Calendar

SPRING If necessary, apply moss killer and about fourteen days afterwards rake up all the winter debris including the dead moss. Use a wire rake so that the lawn is well scarified at the same time and apply the first feed when the grass has started to grow and temperatures are beginning to rise. Mowing should commence at the same time but do not shave the lawn; give it only a gentle trim at first and as growth increases, gradually lower the mower blades over a period of two to three weeks. Continue to feed as spring turns into early summer. If the ground has already been prepared for a new lawn, work the soil into a fine seedbed, apply pre-seeding fertiliser, firm the ground and sow when the soil is moist during the first half of spring.

SUMMER Mow frequently, twice a week during the height of the growing season; keep lawn edges well clipped. Always use the grass box except during periods of exceptional drought when the grass mowings left on the lawn protect the grass from the hot sun. Water whenever necessary and feed at three to four-weekly intervals. Use weedkillers, treat against earthworms and other pests and act immediately to control disease at the very first indication.

AUTUMN Continue mowing as long as the grass is still growing but set the cutting cylinder fairly high so that the turf has some protection from cold winds and severe weather during the winter. Frequently rake up fallen leaves and scatter worm-casts, attend to repairs, dig out coarse grasses and make good; improve sub-surface drainage if necessary.

Aerate the area and follow with a top-dressing which is best combined with an autumn feed unless this has already been given. Tidy up lawn edges. This is an ideal time for turfing and sowing new lawns, as well as seeding freshly repaired patches.

Start cultivating those areas which are intended for new lawns during the following spring.

WINTER Lawns need air; keep them free of rubbish, rake up leaves, and, provided the ground is not frosted nor too wet, continue with aeration. Complete constructional work and level uneven patches.

Avoid walking on very wet, frozen or snow-covered turf.

Attend to the lawn-mower and send it for servicing and re-sharpening.

Appendix 5

Useful Weights, Measures and Conversions

Imperial

LENGTH

1 inch		= 2.54 cm
1 foot	= 12 inches	= 0.3048 m
1 yard	= 3 feet	= 0.9144 m

SURFACE OR AREA

1 sq inch		= 6.4516 cm^2
1 sq foot	= 144 sq inches	= 0.0929 m^2
1 sq yard	= 9 sq ft	= 0.8361 m^2

CAPACITY

1 cu inch		= 16.387 cm^3
1 cu foot	= 1.728 cu inches	= 0.0283 m^3
1 cu yard	= 27 cu feet	= 0.7646 m^3
1 pint	= 20 fl oz	= 0.5683 litres
1 quart	= 2 pints	= 1.1365 litres
1 gallon	= 8 pints	= 4.5461 litres

WEIGHT

1 ounce	= 437$\frac{1}{2}$ grains	= 28.350 gm
1 pound	= 16 ounces	= 0.4536 kg
1 stone	= 14 pounds	= 6.3503 kg

Metric

LENGTH

1 centimetre (cm)	= 10 millimetres	= 0.3937 in
1 metre (m)	= 100 cm	= 1.0936 yd

SURFACE OR AREA

1 sq cm (cm^2)	= 100 mm^2	= 0.155 sq in
1 sq metre (m^2)	= 10,000 cm^2	= 1.196 sq yd
1 are (a)	= 100 m^2	= 119.6 sq yd

CAPACITY

1 cu cm (cm^3)		= 0.061 cu in
1 cu metre (m^3)	= 999.972 litre	= 1.308 cu yd
1 litre (l)	= 1.000028 dm^3	= 1.7598 pints

WEIGHT

1 milligram (mg)		= 0.0154 gram
1 gram (g)	= 1,000 mg	= 0.0353 oz
1 kilogram (kg)	= 1,000 g	= 2.2046 lb
1 tonne (t)	= 10 q	= 0.9842 ton

EQUIVALENT MEASURES

1 oz per sq yd	= 34 g per m^2
1 gall per sq yd	= 5.4 l per sq m

Conversion Factors

TO CONVERT	TO	MULTIPLY BY	RECIPROCAL
Inches (in)	Centimetres (cm)	2.54	0.394
Yards (yd)	Metres (m)	0.914	1.09
Square yards (yd)^2	Square metres (m)^2	0.836	1.20
Pounds (lb)	Kilograms (kg)	0.454	2.20
Gallons (gall)	Litres (l)	4.55	0.22

TEMPERATURE CONVERSION

Celcius (C) = 5/9 F–32°

Farenheit (F) = 9/5 C+32°

Playing Area Measurements

Tennis court	26 x 12 yds	(312 sq yds)
Tennis court, single	26 x 9 yds	(234 sq yds)
Croquet lawn	35 x 28 yds	(980 sq yds)
Bowling green, maximum	44 x 44 yds	(1936 sq yds)
Bowling green, minimum	40 x 21 yds	(840 sq yds)

Acknowledgements

I am most grateful to The Ministry of Agriculture, Fisheries and Food (Agricultural Chemicals Approval Organisation, Harpenden), for permission to reproduce the Agricultural Chemicals approval mark. My special thanks also to Marguerite Miles for the line drawings and to Louise Roberts for so ably arranging and typing the manuscript.

Matt Templeton